Edinburgh's Castle

(Backdrop to 'Hogmanay')

Edinburgh's Castle in the Air

(Backdrop to 'Hogmanay')

ALASTAIR M. R. HARDIE

SERENDIPITY

All photographs by the author, except Figure 57 by Alex Hay

First published in 2004 by
Serendipity
Suite 530
37 Store Street
Bloomsbury
London

British Library Cataloguing-in-Publication data
A catalogue record for this book is available from the British Library
ISBN 1-84394-111-2
Printed and bound by Antony Rowe

To my late wife Helen and my daughter Sheenagh, who were most tolerant and understanding while I was carrying out the research into this my second work. Also to my grandchildren Sarah, Emma and Andrew, all of whom I hope may find this book of interest when they are old enough to understand and appreciate it.

CONTENTS

ILLUSTRATIONS

PROLOGUE

Rome wasn't built – nor was the history of Edinburgh Castle written – in a day!

This is not intended to be a dry historical tome, nor is it meant to be a walking guide to all parts of the Castle; there are many of these, including a CD-Rom Gallery Guide – a personalised audio system. No! Instead it is a record of interesting facts, some little known, gathered at various times over a period of more than forty years: not consistently, I may add, during that time, but as and when the inspiration or the interest took me – it has therefore been 'on simmer' for a lengthy period! History of course comes into it, no detail of such an ancient or important 'monument' could exclude history, but it is interspersed with interesting snippets.

Let me explain how it all commenced… In the mid 1960s I worked in an office in Edinburgh's Lothian Road. Invariably at lunch time I would eat my packed lunch almost within the shadow of the Castle, sitting either above the sunken multi-storey car park in Castle Terrace, or in West Princes Street Gardens.

Naturally my thoughts would wander to days of yore with such questions as: How old is the Castle? Who lived in it? Were any battles fought in close proximity to where I was sitting? Sieges on the rock face? Prisoners taken? Did Royalty play a part? And so on.

It is of course a well known fact that visitors to our city take more of an interest in, and know much more about, such places of historical interest than the local inhabitants do.

My curiosity sufficiently aroused, therefore, I decided to find out as much as I could for my own enlightenment and satisfaction, and so my research – my 'time machine' – commenced. I had the correct atmosphere, position and surroundings in which to read up from borrowed library books and thus formulate most of my basic draft notes, for what must have happened all those years ago. At that time I had no intention of writing a book on the matter: no, as I have said, I just wanted to educate myself and satisfy my own curiosity.

Little did I know that I would discover such curious and interesting facts as for example, how old the Castle rock is; the mystery of the remains of a Royal baby found in a hollow cavity in the wall of the Royal apartments

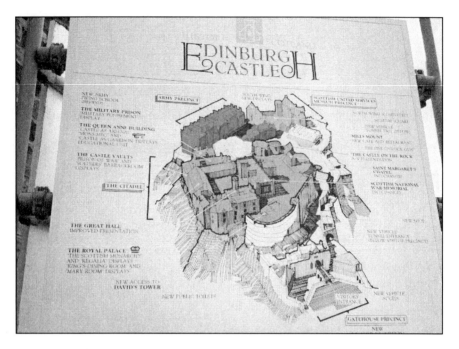

Figure 1. Plan of Edinburgh Castle on display in the precincts

when repairs were being carried out in 1830; the reason for the one o'clock gun being fired every week-day; the amount of water which is contained within the Castle rock; the piece of ground on the Esplanade which belongs to Nova Scotia; or the Memorial in stone to such creatures as mice, canaries, elephants and camels in the Scottish National War Memorial.

It occurred to me that with all the fighting, battles and sieges which took place in this area in those medieval days the Castle must have been regarded as the most prized possession in Scotland by the English Kings and jealously guarded by the Scottish Monarchs – in fact a real trophy!

I chose the book's title because from many viewpoints in Edinburgh the Castle appears to dominate the skyline advantageously and seems to float as if perched in air!

I would hope that the visitor to the Castle whether local or from afar will find that the contents of this book give him or her as much pleasure and interest as it has given me in gathering all the facts together.

The reader will no doubt appreciate that in compiling it its authenticity must not be taken as irrefutable although every care has been taken to make it as accurate as possible.

In conclusion, all Edinburgh citizens should be extremely proud to know that in 1995 the United Nations Educational Scientific and Cultural Organisation designated Edinburgh's Old and New Towns the prestigious title of a 'World Heritage Site'. This in effect puts the centre of the Capital (of which the Castle plays a prominent part) on a parallel with the Colosseum of Rome, the Island of St Kilda and India's Taj Mahal and makes us officially World famous!

No! – Rome wasn't built – nor was the history of Edinburgh Castle written – in a day! ... as you will find out; or as an historian remarked recently: 'It is our job to keep the past alive because the past is a part of now.'

Alastair M. R. Hardie
Edinburgh, 2004

INTRODUCTION

Several hairy men, with the pelts of wild animals clinging to their bodies, stalk cautiously through a dense tangled forest of oak, ash and elm, grown thick, trackless and marshy with alder and willow. The stench of accumulated rotting vegetation, surrounding a stagnant swamp nearby, does not appear to disturb them so intent are they on their prey – a wild ox, driven frenzied with anger, its eyes blinded by sweat and blood which oozes from wounds inflicted by primitive stone spears, slings, clubs and other makeshift weapons. Trapped in a thicket it makes a brave stand. Weakness overcomes it, however, as the hairy creatures close in. Nevertheless in its death throes its flailing hooves cave in the chest of one of the stalwarts and with a resounding crack, splits open the skull of another like a walnut in a nutcracker. Their dying cries send the animals of the forest scurrying to and fro – the timid red and roe deer, an elk being watched and closely followed by a wild boar and pack of wolves; a snorting white-maned wild bull prances about; a mammoth tosses its head back and bellows;[1] otters jump into a straggling stream nearby and a brown bear ambles curiously by. Cranes, grouse, blackcock, capercailzie, a great auk and other lesser birds momentarily darken the sky in their flight.

Soon peace, quiet and dust settle over the gory scene and silence reigns once again broken occasionally by a moan or groan from a dying warrior, left by his companions to join the foetid vegetation.

Later the hairy men can be seen hauling the carcass of the beast, victim of their primitive weapons, up to their rough encampment of turf, bracken, rocks and adobe huts perched high on a rugged bump of rock. From it they look out, on all sides, upon steamy, misty forests which conceal many hidden evils and lurking dangers, and they feel safe – for a while …

Such may have been the daily occurrence many many centuries ago, where now stands Edinburgh's 'Castle in the Air' overlooking famous Princes Street with its picturesque gardens, hard though it may be to visualise from our civilised place in time. Nowadays, the tourist, confronted with the colourful panorama for the first time, experiences an urge to explore, to find out about the Castle and its Rock; to get at the beginnings of this great City's Fortress.

[1] Mammoths are believed to have become extinct at the end of the Ice Age 11,750 years ago and their remains are very rare in Scotland; a tusk of one was found in 1820 and is now on display in the New Museum of Scotland.

CHAPTER ONE

IN THE BEGINNING

Robert Louis Stevenson described the Castle rock as 'Nature's most satisfactory crag'.

Without this magnificent mountain the whole history of Scotland could have been different with the Castle sited elsewhere and the town merely another East Coast nonentity. The rock's powerful presence even shaped the City, holding its residents protectively close for centuries longer than was really necessary and colouring its streets with warring blood and purple pageantry.

This was the magnet that drew attackers from north as well as south of the Border – the prize jackpot for which English kings gambled great armies and Scottish nobles hazarded the kingdom.

But let us first peer through the mists of time …

The old British chroniclers believed that a fortress of some sort existed where Edinburgh Castle now stands, about the time when the Temple of Solomon was built, centuries before the founding of Rome! Edinburgh's history however goes back thirty centuries – thousands of years more than was previously thought.

Archaeological excavations in the Castle in 1988 revealed that the first settlement was established here about 1000 BC. Scanty remnants of Bronze Age buildings – including floors and hearths – were unearthed in an archaeological dig which revealed that Edinburgh is one of the longest inhabited places in Northern Europe. Excavations also recovered considerable quantities of Bronze Age food debris.

The settlement on Edinburgh's great rock continued to prosper through the Iron Age. Iron fragments and shards of pottery from the era were unearthed in the dig as were two shale bangles – items of 2,300 year-old jewellery. The Iron Age inhabitants appear to have been involved in making large numbers of bone items. Lots of bone-working debris has been found.

In the early Roman period the rock settlement grew in importance. The remains of several stone buildings have been discovered, dating from the first and second centuries AD. Roman period finds include decorated glass, fine continental pottery and a dragon-shaped Celtic-style brooch.

In two pits located under a pavement of flat cobbles was discovered what appears to have been a foundation offering – a corn-grind quern and two complete pots. The offering was probably designed to ensure prosperity and good luck for the inhabitants of the house.

The dig also revealed evidence of Dark Age occupation. Until then the only real suggestion that Edinburgh was inhabited at that period came from a late sixth century epic poem which refers to Din Edyn (the fortress of Edin). Before the series of excavations there had been no physical evidence that Edinburgh predated medieval times.

With its natural defences and precipitous rock rising on all sides it was certainly recognised by the military powers of bygone days as being one of the most commanding and valuable positions in the world (as the world was then) and until gunpowder was invented was thought to be impregnable.

But let us pause for a few moments to 'time-travel' back about 350 million years. The area that we are researching was a roaring, erupting, active volcano spewing out molten lava and clouds of burning ash. The Castle Rock and Arthur's Seat were heaving and exploding hundreds of feet higher than the rocky outcrops we know today, ultimately folding and tilting to form our familiar landscape.

The Royal Mile which extends from the Castle to Holyrood was constructed naturally by a ridge of lava which flowed eastwards from the Castle rock eruption.

The old rock is basically basalt. The rugged bump which we can see rising as it does to a height of 435 ft above sea level is only the 'tip of the iceberg'; the basalt goes deep, probably descending for several miles below ground shaped like a cylinder. Originally a volcano, as already mentioned, which failed to remain completely surfaced it has, over its earlier years, forced its way upwards through the earth's crust and has been worn into its present shape and position by glacial action during the Ice Age. The Calton Hill is a similar formation and the two may be connected some distance underground. The naked rocks, however, have now been largely covered by the accumulated soil and overgrowth of centuries and the ascent and access has been correspondingly simplified. And yet it is still a stiff climb. Other remnants of old volcanoes are Blackford Hill, Corstorphine Hill, Traprain Law and North Berwick Law.

The rock and Castle buildings are not only the key to the modern city, they are also the gateway to its romantic past. The story of the Castle is the story of the City's infancy, firstly breathing life into settlements around its walls and then providing a support system for the medieval Old Town stretching down the Royal Mile, allowing the city to grow up into Scotland's capital. It has existed as a stronghold beyond human record of memory.

It is not until about the year 994 BC that we can actually establish that the rock was occupied as a fortified station, in a very rough and modified form, by a British Prince – Cruthenus Camelon, King of the 'Wheat-eaters' and the Picts.

In 989 BC when King Ebranke, son of Mempricius, ruled 'Britayne' he is reputed to have founded Edinburgh besides building York and other places, and had the fortress rebuilt, no doubt to accommodate the 21 wives, 20 sons and 30 daughters he is said to have had!

As a result of frequent wars with the Picts, Danes, Saxons and Romans ownership of the fortress passed rapidly from hand to hand down to the reign of Malcolm II, although, oddly enough, the Roman Legions were never known to have actually occupied it. The eagle eye of the Roman invader, however, could hardly have overlooked this natural stronghold halfway between his two stations on the adjoining sea-coast – Inveresk and Cramond. The latter is believed to have been a third century base camp for the Roman Emperor Septimus Sevenus. He came to Scotland in AD 208 and systematically laid waste to the countryside north of the Forth, killing off hundreds of thousands of Caledonian people by setting fire to their crops and plantations. Records show that an Iron Age settlement on the Castle rock escaped the atrocities by collaborating with the invaders.

With this frequent change of 'landlords' the face of the Castle naturally changed too.

Through time a city grew up in close proximity to the Castle originating mainly from the protection which it offered. When invasion pressed unduly hard the inhabitants sought refuge within its battlements. They were mainly an agricultural people and developed into a trading community providing the Castle dwellers with supplies. A convenient seaport nearby, where Leith is now situated, afforded easy trading access with the outside world.

Down through the ages the Castle has been given many names, some of them far-fetched and fanciful, others more logical.

The ancient Britons called the rock *Mynyd Agned* (or 'Painted Mount'); the Gaels – *Dunedin* (*Oppidum Eden* in the *Latin Chronicle*) or *Din Edyn* (the 'face of the hill' or 'fortress on the slope' or the 'strength of Edwin'), when it was reputed to boast a Great Hall where the warriors of King Mynyddog feasted. Some say it was fortified by the daughters, or nuns, of the Pictish Kings and derived the name of *Castrum Puellarum* ('Castle of the Maidens'), others say that the Gadeni occupied it.

Although the records do not indicate Roman occupation Ptolemy's second century map of the Roman Empire marks the Castle as *Castrum Alatum* because of its supposed similarity to an outspread eagle.

Legend has it that in 1178 the nuns were thrust out by St David, and Canons introduced in their place by the Pope as being more suitable to live amongst soldiers! It has also been called such names as 'The Winged Fort' and 'The Virgins' Castle'.

The derivation of the name EDINBURGH is similarly said to have come from various sources, the most convincing one, although not proved, being that Edwin, greatest of the Northumbrian Kings, who fell at the Battle of Hatfield Chase in Yorkshire in 633 fighting Penda, King of Mercia, is credited with having fortified the city in 626 and of having spent a great deal of his time there.

Earlier in the year 617 Edwin took over the area called Deira (from the Tees to the Humber) and also Bernicia (from the Tees to the Firth of Forth) – known as united Northumbria. Edwinsburgh (or Edwinesburg) was the most northern outpost of this territory. (The oldest form of this name appears in a Charter granted by David I, between 1112 and 1147, after the foundation of the Abbey of Holyrood.)

Edwin's reign was chiefly noted for the introduction of Christianity into Northumbria.

Despite the archaeological evidence mentioned earlier the evidence of the first two thousand years as a fortress is lost in the mists of the Dark Ages.

CHAPTER TWO

THE ROYAL CONNECTIONS

From early times the Castle, as it was then, has either been the residence of, or has had connections with, Royalty.

In 1067 a little party of refugees, fleeing from William the Conqueror who was by then King of England, arrived at a sheltered bay on the Fife coast of the Firth of Forth, since called 'St Margaret's Hope'. Among them was the Anglo-Saxon princess Margaret, great niece of Edward the Confessor, who had been routed in the south. They were seeking the protection of King Malcolm III of Scotland (Malcolm Canmore or as he was known in Gaelic 'Ceann-Mor' – Malcolm of the Big Head) in his capital at Dunfermline. He was son of Duncan, the King murdered by Macbeth.

From their landing place they were ferried, according to legend, on the last stage of their journey to safety and the hospitality of the Scottish king. By all accounts he was a man of power but with little or no learning. The Princess was of some refinement and religious devotion. The King, a widower, readily offered sanctuary and the princess no doubt impressed him. In 1071 they married and so Margaret became Queen of Scotland.

They dwelt mainly in Dunfermline (*Dun-fiar-linne* – the Tower by the Crooked Stream) which in those mid-eleventh century days was the Scottish capital. However, as they spent most of their time in Edinburgh Castle and since the hamlet round its base was growing steadily in importance, Dunfermline was soon ousted from its position as prime town.

'**The Binks**' at what is now South Queensferry, on the Firth of Forth, formed a natural rocky jetty and was a regular landing place for the Queen's Ferry, this being so named since Margaret endowed ships for the free passage of pilgrims and the poor, and also hostels for them on either shore of the Forth. It may be assumed that she used the ferry herself when going between Dunfermline and Edinburgh. It became known as *Passagium Reginae* – the Queen's Passage or Ferry. To mark the 900th anniversary of her death the St Margaret's Chapel Guild erected a stone and plaque at 'The Binks' jetty in 1993.

Margaret was a good and well-loved queen. A deeply religious woman renowned for her piety and sophistication, she helped civilise the Scottish Court, and introduced many religious reforms. She tended the sick and the poor, ensuring that they and their children were well cared for and so brought

Figures 2 and 3. 'The Binks' – indicates the 'Ancient and Modern' being the landing place for the Queen's Ferry which plied between South and North Queensferry and no doubt carried Queen Margaret at times between Dunfermline and Edinburgh Castle. In contrast are the Forth rail and road bridges.

a sense of refinement into their lives. **St Margaret's Chapel**, the oldest building in the Castle, is dedicated to her memory although it was probably not built until after her son David I came to the throne in 1124. Other records however indicate that she founded the chapel. Of Norman design, it is the oldest example of Norman architecture in Scotland and well-preserved to this day; it probably owes its survival and existence to its unique position on the highest pinnacle of the rock.

Figure 4. The Lang Stairs and within Portcullis Gate – the original entrance to the upper enclosure.

The original entrance to the upper enclosure was by means of the **Lang Stairs** beside **Portcullis Gate**. However, an easier entrance to the citadel was created in the seventeenth century in the reign of Charles II (1660-85) when the perimeter wall looped and pierced by a series of openings for cannon and musketry was built. This contained a single gate known mysteriously as **Foog's Gate**, set in a kink in the wall thus enabling it to be covered by flanking fire from the neighbouring wall.

At this stage we can pause to let wartime 'Radio Padre', the late Very Rev. Dr Ronald Selby Wright, former minister of Canongate Kirk, describe his love of St Margaret's Chapel in a brief extract from a small booklet – *St Margaret Queen of Scotland and her Chapel*:

> Queen Margaret was one of the most loved queens there has ever been and she was loved because she herself loved so much. Her little Chapel built so long ago has stood until this day on this very spot where it now stands, a place set apart where in days of siege and war, as well as in days of peace and plenty, people have come to give God their worship – those great in power, those great in humility or just ordinary folk. There they've come, Kings and Queens, lords and ladies, knights and lairds, soldiers of the Cross, brothers and sisters from over the Border and friends from many distant lands.

Though services were always held in the castle it is sad to think that after the Reformation the Chapel was practically forgotten. Possibly the last time it was used by Royalty was during the 3 months residence of Mary Queen of Scots after the murder of David Rizzio. Thereafter the structure disappeared so completely from public knowledge that none of our histories before 1845 refer to it. At that time it was used by the battery of the Castle for storing the gunpowder with which salutes were fired on special occasions.

Figure 5. A view of St Margaret's Chapel through Foog's Gate.

The interior presents much the same appearance as it did in the days of David I. While only 14 ft wide at the west end it is fully 16 ft at the east. The length is about 32 ft. The east windows are off centre and the ornate Chancel Arch, built by David in memory of his mother, is irregularly placed suggesting that the main walls are older than the interior.

In 1853 it was thoroughly renovated, Queen Victoria taking a great interest in the restoration of its pristine beauty, when the five small windows were filled in with stained glass, later to be replaced as we have them now. In 1929 by the vision, action and generosity of the late Sir David Russell a start was made to restore it not only to its former glory but to something of its former use. In 1934 the restored and re-furnished Chapel was dedicated.

In 1942 the St Margaret's Chapel Guild was started under the patronage of HRH Princess Margaret (who was 12 at the time) to arrange that those with the name of Margaret should supply and place flowers in the Chapel each week of the year to keep the life and principles of St Margaret before Scottish women and girls as an example of good and Christian womanhood and to encourage use of the Chapel as often as possible for public and private devotions.

Figure 6. St Margaret's Chapel – The highest and oldest building in the Castle

More additions to the interior are the small stained glass portrayals of the Saints – Margaret, Ninian, Columba and Andrew. To some it may be that a small framed reproduction on the Chapel interior wall, showing an open page of St Margaret's Gospel Book (the original is in the Bodliean Library, Oxford) with a medieval style figure balanced by lines of fine script, gets nearer than anything else on view to illustrate the civilising influence brought to Edinburgh by the Queen of Scots who became a Saint. It is sad to relate that in 1093 when Malcolm and his eldest son Edward were both slain at the Battle of Alnwick, Margaret lay dying in her sick bed within the Castle. News of their deaths hastened her own end and she died broken-hearted with the Black Rood of Scotland pressed to her brow.

Soon after Malcolm's and Margaret's deaths Donald Bane, Malcolm's younger brother, in exile in the Highlands, having heard of Malcolm's death, raised a fierce band of hairy Highlanders, clad in dun-deer's hide, and descended upon the Castle in an attempt to claim the throne – the first recorded siege of the Castle. In those days no mercy could be expected, torture and pillage being the order of the day. The entrance to the Castle must always have been at the same place as today although in former times the approach was by a flight of steps on the northern side known as the **Lang Stairs**. In the Highland band's eagerness to capture the impregnable fortress they mounted guards at the base of three of its sides but left the steep western side of the rock unguarded. At dead of night, and engulfed by a 'miraculous' mist, the Queen's body was lowered down the steep scarp on the west leading to St Cuthbert's Church and escorted via 'Queen's' Ferry to Dunfermline Abbey where she was laid to rest in the very place which she herself had founded. It was not until about a century and a half later that she was canonised in 1250.

On the 900th anniversary of her death in 1993 Historic Scotland issued a brief pamphlet – The Story of St Margaret 1047-1093. An extract from it reads:

There was once a Princess called Margaret, which means 'the pearl'. She was born an exile in Hungary, daughter of a Saxon Prince and a Hungarian Princess. When Margaret's father came home to England she was brought up at the court of the pious and learned king, Edward the Confessor. There for the first time she met Malcolm of Scotland who had fled from the murderous clutches of Macbeth.

When Edward died without an heir, confusion and war followed. The new king, Harold, was killed at Hastings by William the Conqueror. A fugitive once more, Margaret set sail for Hungary but was driven by a storm to the shores of Scotland. Malcolm, now King of Scots, came to meet her. He fell in love and asked Margaret to become his Queen.

Longing for the peace and holy quiet of the cloister, Margaret hesitated to marry the warrior king. Then she became Malcolm's wife and Scotland's Queen.

From the beginning she opened her arms to the people. Orphans were taken into the Royal palace, the sick and the suffering tended, prisoners of war released, and the poorest fed. For Malcolm Margaret could do no wrong. He supported her work and rewarded those who followed her example. He would take her precious books in his hands, turning over the pages and kissing them. Once he sent for a jeweller to ornament a book with gold and gems. Then he gave it to Margaret as a token of his love. The Royal couple had 2 daughters and 6 sons whose upbringing was Margaret's special concern. But she also had a secret life of prayer. From the palace at Dunfermline she would retreat to a cave to be alone with God and at Edinburgh Malcolm built a Chapel for her devotions. This extraordinary Queen lived the ideal of inward poverty.

After her death she left a new sense of human kindness and a religious inspiration to Scotland. Pilgrims crossed the Forth to St Andews on the Queen's Ferry. Through her influence monks once more worshipped on Iona after the ravages of the Vikings. In time she became a Saint and her own church at Dunfermline became a great Abbey and place of pilgrimage. Three of her sons were among the greatest kings who ever ruled Scotland and Britain's present Royal Family is descended from Margaret.

Queen Margaret's youngest son (her eighth child), David I, founder of Holyrood Abbey, having inherited his mother's piety, resided in the Castle at a time when it knew peace. His example was followed by his successors Malcolm IV, William the Lion who surrendered the Castle on becoming a vassal of Henry II of England (in 1174 – the first recorded occupation by the English enemy) and Alexander II. The Castle remained an English garrison for nearly fifteen years until 1189.

Alexander III and his Queen, Margaret (daughter of Henry III of England), lived within the precincts of the Castle during their long and prosperous reign making the building famous not only as a Royal residence but also as a respected seat of justice. Unfortunately, Alexander III's descendant died unmarried and the line with the throne was broken.

Figure 7. Inside St Margaret's Chapel – Notice the flowers placed weekly in the Chapel by those with name of Margaret.

A dark period for Scottish history followed – a period of lengthy struggle between Robert Bruce, John Balliol (nicknamed the 'Toom Tabard' or 'Empty Coat') and others, for succession to the throne. Edward I of England, who was responsible for taking the Stone of Destiny from Scone to London, stepped in to take the opportunity of placing the weak John Balliol on the throne as his vassal. But his reign was brief.

After a short siege in 1296, which lasted for eight days, the Castle, attacked with battering rams, once

Figure 8. Dunfermline Abbey – Queen Margaret's final resting place.
(Note the words Bruce and King at the top of the tower.)

again fell, and remained in English hands for seventeen years, during which time Scotland battled for her independence under outlawed William Wallace and King Robert the Bruce.

The English were eventually driven back over the Border but Scotland could not be declared free until the English-held garrisons of Edinburgh, Roxburgh and Stirling Castles had been recaptured. With this in mind Bruce ordered his nephew, Sir Thomas Randolph of Strathdon, first Earl of Moray, to besiege and capture the Castle in March 1312.

What might appear to some to be comparatively modern tactics were adopted - surprise assault being the obvious answer although how this was to be achieved against a fortress which was impregnable on three sides by sheer precipices and so well guarded on the fourth, was in itself a vast hurdle to be overcome.

Sir Randolph chose a band of thirty men and decided to carry out the assault of an unguarded precipitous side one pitch black night. One of his men, a William Francis, had some local knowledge of the area having previously spent some time in the Castle in his young days. Forbidden to leave it he had managed to carry on a courtship with a Scots lass from the township below by finding his way out of the Castle at night, scaling the rampart wall and descending the treacherous rock on the south side, returning by the same route. His knowledge was therefore invaluable for Sir Randolph's purpose.

Determined and undaunted the thirty men slowly made the ascent and out of the murky darkness clambered over the 12 ft high rampart wall. Their surprise attack was successful and Edward's last stronghold in Scotland was shattered. Near the present **Argyll Tower** today, a tablet marks the spot where the brave ascent was made.

On being advised of the achievement King Robert Bruce gave immediate orders for all the buildings ('baith tour and wall') on the Castle Rock, with the exception of **St Margaret's Chapel**, to be demolished ('rycht to the ground') so that they should provide no future shelter in the event of the English ever again securing possession. However on his deathbed in 1329 Bruce spoke of the story of Queen Margaret and her lonely Chapel on the desolate rock and he ordered that it be repaired forthwith, allocating some 40 pounds Scots for that purpose.[2]

The wall at the place where Randolph's Scots clambered up on ladders in 1312 was about 12 ft high and within the enclosure were houses. Twenty-

---

[2] Scottish Currency.
  2 pennies=1 bodle. 2 bodles = 1 plack
  3 bodles = 1 bawbee. 2 bawbees = 1 shilling.
  13 shillings 4 pence = 1 mark. 20 shillings = 1 pound

three years later the only buildings standing on the rock were the Chapel, a little penthouse or lean-to above the Chapel and a new stable of which only a quarter was roofed.

For several years the Rock remained a Scottish possession, then it changed hands again. In 1335 Edward III took it over from David II (Bruce's son) who fled with his Queen to France. The new occupant ordered the fortifications to be rebuilt as one of a series designed to keep the south of Scotland in subjection and then boasted that the new Castle could not be taken by force.

The Black Knight of Liddesdale, Sir William Douglas, planned differently however and by clever scheming outwitted the English and recaptured it in 1341 by a trick – a stratagem on which the old chroniclers love to dwell. The story is too well known to be told in detail.

The plan was devised by Douglas and others. Disguised as merchants bringing corn and wine for sale to the garrison, a party of armed men contrived to overturn their casks and hampers at the gates in such a way as to prevent the guards from closing the barriers. Joined by others who lay concealed close at hand, they attacked the garrison and captured the fortress, again destroying it. The Castle area was back in Scottish hands once more and so it was to remain for the next three centuries, until Cromwell's time.

In 1357 David II returned from captivity in England after an unsuccessful invasion of that land. Seeing that the Castle had worn badly with time and the many batterings it had received during the wars, he gave orders for the building of a new Castle. The walls were strengthened and over a period of ten years a massive keep 60 ft high, with a wall sunk to over 80 ft deep, overlooking the City, known as '**David's Tower**' was built, part of which still exists. The government of Scotland was conducted from this tower in the fourteenth century and David resided within its walls until his death in 1371. A feature of it is a gunhole 18 ft in depth which gives an indication of the thickness of the wall that looks straight down across the **Esplanade** and on to the Royal Mile beyond.

The Castle was so well fortified at this time that the garrison repelled a week's siege by Henry IV with apparent ease.

In 1385 Richard II thought he'd try a siege on the Castle with a large army. He succeeded in burning Edinburgh but his men were driven from the Castle ramparts. As a result of this arson the inhabitants of Edinburgh were permitted to build their houses within the Castle walls.

In certain Charters of 1384/85 regarding the Castle the Abbot of Holyrood was granted by Robert II a site for a house to which he and his

Figure 9. Plaque in memory of Mary of Lorraine.

canons with their household could betake themselves in peace and war. The site was to be beyond the position of the King's 'manor' – apparently David's Tower. Another Charter by John, Earl of Carrick, afterward Robert III, gave free entry and exit with goods and victuals to all and sundry of the Burgesses of Edinburgh and their heirs who had, or wished to have in future, houses in the Castle. Obviously it was in the main an enclosure within which houses could be provided not only for the Abbey household but for the whole burgess population and their servants. Full use was made of timber, wattle and clay building material in constructing parts of the Castle.

In the late 1300s Queen Annabella organised a jousting tournament at the Castle. Twelve knights made it to the final which was won by David, Duke of Rothesay. The Royal sports was a huge success and an Edinburgh tradition was born. Knights were dismembered or beheaded and it was common for the horses to die of their wounds. The tradition continued until the mid-1650s when Oliver Cromwell ruled it unseemly.

In the ensuing years the Castle was used as a dwelling place by a succession of Stuart monarch minors who managed to oppress 'take-over' bids by various powerful families.

James II, III, IV and V (the last with his wife Mary of Lorraine,[3] mother of Mary Queen of Scots) resided for short times within the fortress walls in

---

[3] **Mary of Lorraine**, Queen of James V, mother of Mary Queen of Scots and Regent of Scotland from 1554 to 1560, died in the Castle on 11 June 1560. She was known as 'A lady of honourable conditions, full of humanity, a great lover of justice and helpful to the poor'.

rapid succession between the years 1437 and 1542.

The **Great Hall** has been the scene of many state banquets and dinners to record special occasions. Until 1640 the Scottish Parliament met there. In 1440 during the reign of the young James II, who lived in the Castle, two brothers, William, young Earl of Douglas, and his younger brother David were lured to a banquet in the Great Hall by Crichton and Livingstone, the King's regents. The Douglases were feared as rivals to the Crown. During the dinner when a black bull's head was placed before the brothers – a symbol of death – they were surrounded, dragged from the hall, swiftly tried and beheaded. The meal was afterwards referred to as the Black Dinner. After this murder the Castle was besieged by the Douglas party. The siege lasted nine months followed by the Castle's surrender.

After James IV was killed at Flodden (1513) with nine thousand of his men the frightened local inhabitants built Flodden Wall which commenced at David's Tower.

The reign of the next monarch – Mary Queen of Scots – is known to most people. As a girl of 19 she was welcomed to her dwelling place in the Castle.

Figure 10. The tablet carved in stone with the interlocked letters M & H (Mary & Henry) – public recognition that they had produced an heir.

On 19 June 1566 she gave birth in the Royal apartments to a child – a Prince and heir to two kingdoms, James VI of Scotland and, as he was to become, James I of England. The time was 10.00 a.m. but the Royal Consort Henry Stuart, the worthless and estranged Lord Darnley, did not visit the Queen in the oddly-shaped little bedchamber for at least four hours. Legend has it that the delayed visit plus the Queen's assurance that he was positively the infant's father, suggests Darnley had his doubts. It was only five months earlier that Mary's confident and foreign secretary Rizzio (or Riccio) had been stabbed to death because of his too-close-for-comfort relationship with Mary.

A tablet carved in stone over the arch of the old doorway shows an interlocked

M and H with the date 1566 – public recognition that Mary and Henry had produced an heir. The initials of mother and son surmounted by a crown adorn the roof panels of the little bedchamber. Also seen is the coat-of-arms of the Royal House of Stuart, with the verse being a prayer for divine blessing on the infant Prince as future King of Scotland.

But had Rizzio been the father, and had the discovery that the Queen was pregnant been the reason why the jealous Darnley and some of his lords had disposed of Rizzio?

Queen Mary's bedchamber was at the south-east end of the Tower building, one floor above the level of the parade square. Its windows overlooked the steep rock face which led down to the Grassmarket. The significance of this was the sheltered link it provided with the outside world and as the old, possibly erroneous, story goes, Mary's infant was lowered in a basket by rope down the cliff to be taken to the Roman Catholic stronghold of Stirling Castle to be baptised in that faith. Although the Reformation had established the Protestant Church six years earlier, Queen Mary was a devout and defiant Roman Catholic.

The story, as it goes, was straightforward. The infant was only a day or two old when the plan was made. The problem was fitting in the trip to and from Stirling between the short period of darkness in those summery days. Heavy rain clouds, however, brought darkness early that night and the mission got off to a fast start.

After the basket was lowered the rope was rewound and hidden in a chest in the Queen's bedchamber to await the signal to lower it, when the journey had been completed, to the grassy slopes leading to the Grassmarket.

Before dawn, the ceremony performed, the infant was taken back to Edinburgh from Stirling and raised by basket to the bedchamber. Some elaborate versions of the clandestine baptism soon replaced the simple version.

When eight months later Darnley was murdered at Kirk o'Fields near Holyrood, suspicion about the infant's father grew. It was then that Mary committed the infant to the care of the Earl of Mar and was taken captive, although not unwillingly on her part, by the Protestant Earl of Bothwell, another unworthy character of bad reputation. He detained her at Dunbar Castle before they travelled to Edinburgh Castle to await Bothwell's divorce before they could marry.

As the years went on the Earl of Mar raised the youngster as a son. People noted that they had similar features, the young James inheriting none of the delicate features of either parent.

Figures 11, 12 and 13. Painted details
from the Queen's bedchamber

And so it was to remain – nothing more than an old story based on supposition for over 2½ centuries, until ... A veil of suspected Royal mystery shrouds the Castle walls – in August 1830 while repairs were being carried out on the west front of the Royal apartments an interesting discovery was made. A hollow cavity was located and when it was opened from the outside it revealed a recess, 2 ft 6 inches by 1 foot, which contained an ancient oak coffin much decayed and bearing the remains of an infant wrapped in a woollen cloth, very thickly woven to resemble leather. This garment covered the decayed fragments of a richly embroidered silk cloth which bore two initials, one of which was an 'I'.

The discovery was reported to General Thackery, commanding the Royal Engineers at the Castle at the time. He ordered that the tiny crypt in the wall be resealed. Could this have been the remains of the infant who should have succeeded to the throne as James I and who possibly died shortly after birth?

Could this baby have been replaced by the infant taken from Stirling Castle and raised by rope to the Royal apartments? And was the baby raised up the cliff the infant son of the Earl of Mar?

As far as is known, the remains still lie within the walls of the Royal apartments. Scientific examination of the remains might prove or completely discount these stories. But perhaps it is better that we do not know ... after all, why spoil a good story for a few facts?

Figure 14. The Forewall Battery

Mary's connection with the Castle was therefore shortened – she was captured by Confederate Lords and her year-old son was crowned James VI at Stirling (and James I of England after the death of Queen Elizabeth in 1603). The country was divided into two parties – those who followed the new King and those who paid allegiance to the Queen. Among the latter was Sir William Kirkcaldy of Grange, probably the most famous of the long line of Governors of the Castle. On behalf of his Queen he carried out a five year long defence of the Castle against overwhelming odds. This ended in 1573. He and his men were declared rebels and traitors by the King's party and Queen Elizabeth of England was asked for military assistance to take his garrison prisoners.

Kirkcaldy's defensive tactics of repairing the Castle walls, fortifying the approaches and mounting additional cannon, paid dividends and were so effective that the King's party was forced to retire. A further army of 2,000 men and heavy artillery was sent back to ask for his surrender; his reply was to lower the national flag of St Andrew and in its place hoist a scarlet banner on **David's Tower**, a symbol of death and defiance signalling resistance to the last.

War was the only alternative.

Heavy cannon was spaced ominously at intervals round the rock and for three days continuous cannonade was maintained – the severest bombardment the old fortress had ever suffered in its long history. The Castle towers were badly damaged, falling masonry put many guns out of action and the water supply was cut off when David's Tower collapsed on to the well. The water supply was then supplemented from the well near the base of the rock on the north side now known as **St Margaret's Well**. This spring was drawn upon but had been poisoned by the besiegers which resulted in an outbreak of sickness among the garrison. When all hope of escape was blocked havoc resulted and mutiny prevailed.

Kirkcaldy, seeing that he was defeated but not wishing to surrender the Castle to the English army, handed it over to the commander of the blockading Scottish troops of the King's party. Although he pleaded pitifully to Queen Elizabeth he was ordered to be executed and his head hung on the wall of the Castle which he had defended so bravely.

Kirkcaldy was renowned as 'Scotland's most gallant and chivalrous soldier' having held the Castle against tremendous odds defending the cause of a Scottish Queen who had been an exile from the country of her birth – a cause which was now lost forever.

A plaque in his memory exists on the lower wall of the **Forewall Battery**[4] and reads:

> *In memory of Sir William Kirkcaldy of Grange justly reputed to be one of the best soldiers and most accomplished cavaliers of his time. He held this Castle for Queen Mary from May 1568 to May 1573 and after its honourable surrender suffered death for devotion to her cause on 3 August 1573.*

Figure 15. Death Mask of Mary Queen of Scots in Jedburgh Museum

But what became of Mary? Her fate was sealed by her cousin Queen Elizabeth I.

Directly or indirectly Mary had been involved in plots against Elizabeth, in plans for Catholic rebellion and in Continental diplomatic intrigues. Imprisoned for nineteen years in England she had symbolised the aspirations of European Catholics who had hoped to see her replace the Virgin Queen.

Believing there was a threat of foreign invasion the English government was persuaded that, to ensure political stability, Mary could not be allowed to live.

[4] **Forewall Battery** was built by King James V on the line of the medieval defences; the guns were made about 1810.

Figure 16. The Esplanade and approach view of the castle

Eventually Elizabeth agreed and gave the order for Mary to die under the executioner's axe at Fotheringay Castle in 1587.

Her death mask can be seen in Queen Mary's House in Jedburgh – it serves as a museum containing relics associated with the Queen.

Although born in a small room above the most precipitous part of the Castle rock Mary's son James VI had little other connection with the Castle although his name is associated with a series of regrettable incidents which took place within the Castle and its immediate precincts, and earned him the title of 'Hammer of the Witches'. At his command men and women were burned at the stake after they had been found guilty of witchcraft. Others were tortured by various methods – a twisted cord bound and tightened round the forehead; fingernails torn out with pincers; needles thrust into fingers until their heads disappeared; legs crushed in boots until 'blood and marrow spouted forth'. This Royal interest in witchcraft nurtured an intense enthusiasm in such 'sport' which was to last for over a century and take an average toll of about 500.

The Esplanade. Early in the seventeenth century King Charles I took possession of the lands which later became Nova Scotia in Canada. He was keen to develop the territory, the only problem being that he didn't have enough

Figure 17. "Nova Scotian" land on the Esplanade

money. He therefore decided to raise cash by creating two hundred estates in Nova Scotia to sell off to Scottish noblemen. The new owners would then be made baronets.

When land or property was sold under Scottish law at that time the deal was concluded by the seller handing over a piece of earth from the property. This caused a problem however as Charles didn't want to travel all the way to Nova Scotia. To get round it he made a Royal Proclamation stating that Nova Scotia was incorporated with the Kingdom of Scotland. Edinburgh Castle was the most famous place in Scotland so during a brief visit to the Castle the King declared earth and stone from the Castle Esplanade (which was at a much lower level than today) to be Nova Scotian soil and could be used for the ceremony instead.

So it was there that 64 of the new landowners became baronets, a transaction which brought in some much needed money to the King's coffers. Today Canadian visitors will no doubt feel very much on 'home ground' when visiting the Castle!

A plaque on the Esplanade wall highlights the event and reads:

Near this spot in 1625 Sir William Alexander of Menstrie, Earl of Stirling received Sasine or Lawful Possession of the Royal Province of Nova Scotia by the Ancient and Symbolic Ceremony of Delivery of Earth and Stone

Figure 18. Disused Fountain on the Esplanade near the site where many witches were burned at the stake

from Castlehill by a Representative of the King. Here also (1625-1637) the Scottish Baronets of Nova Scotia received Sasine of their Distant Baronies.

Although the current Esplanade was used for drilling the garrison of the Castle, being constructed between 1816 and 1820, in early times weird scenes were enacted here – the beheading of traitors, real or supposed, the torturing of 'heretics' and the burning of witches and wizards as has already been mentioned.

A disused fountain at the north side of the entrance to the Esplanade carries the following inscription:

This fountain designed by John Duncan is near the site on which many witches were burned at the stake. The wicked head and serene head signify that some used their exceptional knowledge for evil purposes while others were misunderstood and wished their kind nothing but good. The serpent was the dual significance of evil and wisdom. The foxglove spray further emphasises the dual purpose of many common objects.

The last witch to be burned alive at the stake on the Esplanade was Agnes Finnie in 1643 after thumbscrews had been applied to make her confess before trial, although what she appears to have been accused of was little more than bad temper!

Figure 19. Statue to Field Marshal Earl Haig on the Esplanade

From the Esplanade the line of the Old Town wall can be marked, rising from the south-west corner of the Grassmarket. By this line of the Town Wall is the most impressive view of the Castle, and one seldom seen by the visitor – or the town dweller for that matter.

The equestrian statue on the north side of the Esplanade is of Field Marshal Earl Haig, Commander in Chief of the BEF in France and Belgium during World War I.

Also on the north side of the Esplanade are monuments:

1. To the memory of the Officers, NCOs and men of the Scottish Horse killed in action or died of wounds in the South African War 1901-2.

2. To the memory of the Officers, NCOs and men of the 72nd Duke of Albany's Own Highlanders killed in action or died of wounds or disease during the campaign in Afghanistan 1878-80.

3. A statue to Field Marshal His Royal Highness Frederick Duke of York and Albany KG C-in-C British Army – MDCCCXXVII.

Also on the south side of the Esplanade:

To the memory of the Officers and men of the Gordon Highlanders who lost their lives in the South African War 1899-1902.

In 1650 Charles II (known as 'The Merry Monarch') made a brief visit to the Castle and became the last monarch to enter it until George IV came in 1822. It was after the latter's visit that Sir Walter Scott put forward proposals to open the Castle to the public. These were adopted in the 1850s. His suggestion was perhaps not surprising when it is remembered that following his death the author's Border home, Abbotsford, was the first famous house to be opened to the public, setting a trend for the growing 'stately homes' business.

James IV and V were largely instrumental in transferring the Royal Castle into the majestic palace we enjoy today. During the reign of Queen Anne (in which the Parliamentary Union between Scotland and England of 1707 occurred) a large barracks for Officers

Figure 20. Statue to Field Marshal HRH Frederick Duke of York & Albany on the Esplanade.

Figure 21. Dog cemetery

was erected on the citadel (now the home of the **National War Museum of Scotland**). There has however been a military presence in the form of a garrison or guard at the Castle from the earliest days of the fortress.

From about 1661 the garrison was provided by the Castle Company, which was strengthened in times of crisis by troops from other Scottish regiments, notable among them being the Scots Guards. The Castle Company was replaced by a Veterans' company, and finally by regular infantry units.

In 1794 the barrack blocks were built and these became the established quarters of Infantry units stationed in Edinburgh, until Redford Barracks were completed after the First World War.

In the summer of 1857 daily news came from India of murder and cruelty where native soldiers had mutinied and killed British officers, their wives and children. The 78 Regiment (Seaforth Highlanders) stationed in the Castle at the time was ordered to Bombay to fight the rebels. They mostly spoke Gaelic which few Edinburgh folk understood and were nicknamed 'The Wild Macraas' because years before they themselves had rebelled against their officers and had marched to the top of Arthur's Seat defying anyone to shift them. After a very long sea voyage they entered the thick of the fighting. Of the eight hundred men who left the Castle fewer than half survived. A monument was raised on the north side of the Esplanade to mark this tragic event in memory of the Officers, NCOs and private soldiers of the LXXVIII Highland Regiment who fell in the suppression of the Mutiny of the Native Army of India in the years MDCCCLVII and MDCCCLVIII.

Until the nineteenth century the Castle had been designed to be impregnable – a symbol of military might – but in the mid-1800s a Col. R. C. Moody (O/C Royal Engineers, North Britain) and architect F. T. Dollman felt that it should be turned into a monument to Britain's prosperity. As a result they drew up plans for a romantic Scottish Baronial type/French chateau style castle with several turrets. Queen Victoria was approached and accepted the proposal with enthusiasm. The plan never got off the ground however. In 1861 Prince Albert died and the grieving Queen's initial enthusiasm waned. Later, in 1864, architect David Bryce suggested a massive keep be erected on top of the Castle as a memorial to Albert. The Queen, having lost all heart for the matter, disapproved the plan.

And so the Castle still appears as an impressive impregnable fortress to this day.

With so many regiments and officers in the Castle barracks over the years many had regimental mascots and pet dogs and it was inevitable that a few of the pets would die during their period of service. In a small enclosure within the Castle is a specially constructed **Dog Cemetery** with little gravestones on which are carved the dogs' names. The first one was buried there about 1847, during Queen Victoria's reign (1837-1901).

One of the dogs was 'Pat VC' who followed the 72nd Highlanders in peace and war and saved his master, a colour-sergeant, during the Afghan War. When he was attacked by an Afghan, Pat 'bit him [the assailant] on the calf of the leg', for which he was rewarded the Dickin Medal. He died in 1887.

Another – 'Bob' of the Scots Fusilier Guards – took part in the Crimean War. He 'chased the cannonballs and often burned his nose on a hot one'. He was awarded a special silver medal but was run over by a butcher's cart outside Buckingham Palace. Later he was stuffed and put in a glass case.

During World War II 'Major' (born in December 1941) was a German Shepherd dog sent to war as an RAF Police patrol dog attached to a US Infantry Regiment. Along with his handler he braved Nazi machine-gun fire, air attacks and tank bombardment. On 15 August 1944 'Major' landed on a beach near Cannes with the US 7th Army as 400,000 Allied troops opened a second front in Southern France. The fearless pup was there as the Allies punched their way through Hitler's European underbelly – right at the front, facing fierce enemy resistance every day. He went on all manner of missions – running messages, laying telephone cables and crossing minefields. 'Major' survived the war and returned to his home in Portobello as a hero. He received a special commendation certificate (the animal equivalent of the VC) which read:

> *In grateful recognition of the tireless effort, bravery and constant devotion to duty willingly rendered to Britain and all the free peoples of the world in time of war. From Provost Marshal, Chief of the Royal Air Force Police.*

When he died (in March 1956) at the old age of almost 15 the RAF insisted he be buried like a proper war hero with a full military funeral. He was entered into a grave at the Castle in a special coffin.

Animals have always played a huge role in the defence of the nation (see mention in Chapter 12 relating to the heads carved in stone in the Scottish National War Memorial). The British army has 1,700 dogs. Several thousand dogs served in every Allied theatre of war during World War II in roles too dangerous for human servicemen.

Coat of Arms. Edinburgh has been a Royal Burgh since granted by King Robert Bruce in 1329 and its Coat of Arms was first formally granted by the Lord Lyon in 1732.

The original arms resembled the earliest known seals of the city with Edinburgh Castle on its rock, in silver and black with red flags flying. An anchor crest above the shield signifies the title of Admiral of the Forth held by the Lord Provost.

The shield is held by two supporters – the right hand side being the deer of St Giles, the City's Patron Saint, and the left side supported by a young woman said to represent the legend that in ancient days, the Pictish kings used to shut up their daughters inside the Castle for safety (see page 6 – 'Castle of the Maidens').

Above the anchor was the motto *Nisi Dominus Frustra* – 'Except the Lord in Vain' – which has been associated with the Capital since 1647.

Earlier in the twentieth century, although the exact date is unknown, a helmet with black and silver mantling was added to the Arms and this was used by Edinburgh Town Council. When local government reorganisation came along in 1975 the helmet disappeared and a coronet of three thistles took its place as the standard sign for all new district councils.

In 1996 a further alteration took place when the flower of Scotland 'withered and died', the thistles being replaced by a coronet representing the ancient turreted walls of the City, topping the armorial insignia.

Between 1993 and 1998 an extensive piece of architectural detective work took place to restore an historic suite of rooms – the Royal apartments, Laigh Hall and the King's Presence Chamber – to their former full glory to show how they would have looked for the 'homecoming' of James VI in 1617 on his only visit to Scotland after the Union of the Crowns. By the 1660s they had unfortunately been taken over by the Army and were turned into store-rooms and were more recently used as a tearoom for visitors. Apart from stone fireplaces, door cases and a little room where Mary Queen of Scots gave birth to James VI, nothing had remained of the suite of rooms' former grandeur; instead visitors had been met with something of a disappointment faced with plain painted walls and light modern cornice.

Then serious research to restore the Royal apartments started in 1993. By using the pattern on a small piece of plaster frieze the team of architects picked up clues about the style and quality of the interior designs used to decorate the former apartments. And by visiting buildings from a similar period and of a like status Historic Scotland managed to build up a picture of the plasterwork as well as the joinery, ironmongery, decorating and even style of the light fittings likely to have been used.

Today the decoration of the rooms as they may typically have been in James VI's time gives visitors a real sense of period, setting and grandeur; in fact rooms fit for a king!

For those interested in the lineage of all the Scottish Monarchs from the Unification of Scotland to the Union of the Crowns of Scotland and England and of the English Sovereigns mentioned in this book a list is given in the Appendix.

CHAPTER THREE

MAJOR SIEGES UPON THE CASTLE

As we are aware the Castle has been a place of defence since ancient times – steep crags to the north, south and west kept even the most determined enemies at bay.

Mention has already been made of several minor sieges, the first recorded one being by Donald Bane in 1093 (see page 11) and a famous major one, described in some detail in the last chapter (pages 21–2), which lasted for five years ending in 1573. It is interesting to note that for three hundred years after David's Tower came crashing down during that siege its existence was virtually unknown.

In 1574 the present 'Half Moon Battery' – or in earlier times as it was more picturesquely called, 'The Great Half Bastion Round' – which overlooks the Esplanade and commands the only entrance to the Castle, was erected in place of David's Tower although enough of the ruins survive to indicate a great solid tower-house. This changed the appearance of the Castle rock so much that it is hardly possible to visualise the previous layout of it apart from old drawings.

(In 1912 three members of a Royal Commission on Ancient Monuments excavated below the Half Moon Battery and, to their amazement and delight, came upon a substantial portion of David's Tower. The lower part of the fourteenth century keep was found to be intact, the walls rising to a height of 40 ft. The doorway and well worn steps of the original entrance were discovered and the hall was in a good state of repair.)

There is a fourteenth century **Fore Well** at the Half Moon Battery 110 ft deep and having a capacity of about 28,500 gallons – the ancient source of the Castle's water supply. Visitors from around the world throw, amongst other numerous items, coins of all denominations into the Well for luck. The Well is cleared out about every 5 years.

Until a few years ago the Half Moon Battery contained modern guns for saluting purposes only and from it a gun was fired at 1 p.m. every day (except Sundays). These functions are now carried out from the **Mills Mount Battery** – but more of the background to this later.

One ghostly myth about the Castle is that in 1650 a sentry on duty heard

Figure 22. Part of the Half Moon Battery

the slow beat of a drum on the Esplanade. After receiving no answer to his 'Halt, who goes there?' he fired his musket. Afterwards nothing was found. This haunting drumbeat accompanied by the spectre of a headless drummer was repeated on several occasions afterwards and was thought to be a forecast of war (see Chapter 5.)

Soon after this ghostly drumbeat had been heard the second siege of any significance in the Castle's history had a most unusual twist to it. Instead of bloody battle it was carried out, to a certain extent, by correspondence alone, the pen proving mightier than the sword.

But to start at the beginning: it was the year – already mentioned – 1650 …

Oliver Cromwell and his army had tried to enter Edinburgh but the Scots army, under the command of General David Leslie, had held him at bay causing him to retire to Dunbar.

This manoeuvre however, was later found to be the spider enticing the fly!

Leslie followed with his 22,000 men to Cromwell's 11,000 and suffered a crowning and unexpected defeat. The Scots army was routed, 3,000 were killed and 10,000 taken prisoner for a total loss of 30 of the English army!

Figures 23 and 24. The Half Moon Battery and the Palace

Edinburgh had no defence now and a triumphant Cromwell entered the City to direct operations against King Charles II for almost a year.

His first task, and to his dismay he found it was no easy one, was to wrest the Castle from the grasp of those who held it in the King's name. He commenced his silent siege without delay.

The subject of his first letter to the Castle was about religion. Inside its walls were many refugees from the town, amongst them the ministers of various churches. Cromwell offered them their freedom if they would return to their parishes and preach as he wished. They refused. After a few more exchanges of the

Figure 25. View from the Half Moon Battery towards the Esplanade.

written word he left them alone and concentrated on staffing the churches with lay preachers – his own officers. He even preached himself – in St Giles Cathedral. The local people flocked to hear him and, strangely enough, were pleased with what they heard.

Figure 26. View from the Half Moon Battery towards Princes St and the Scott Monument.

The siege continued. Anyone found trying to contact the inmates of the Castle was tortured; one man was strung up by his thumbs, lighted matches were placed between his fingers and he was burned to the bone.

Seeing that he was making no progress Cromwell ordered some East Lothian miners to excavate 60 yards into the Castle rock, on the south side, in the hope that he could blow up the fortress. This project fell through. A further series of letters requested the Governor to surrender his keep. He replied stating that he must first consult with King Charles – this Cromwell would not permit.

The correspondence continued and eventually on Christmas Eve, on terms favourable to the defenders, the Castle fell into the hands of the English Parliamentary General, who controlled it until his death in 1660.

The third famous siege of the Castle, in 1689, lasted for three months and equalled the one of 1573 for military prowess and dramatic setting. James VII of Scotland and II of England was very keen that Edinburgh should show more respect to his commands and also that Scotland should be come a Roman Catholic country. In Edinburgh a Convention of Estates (not a Parliament, since it had not been summoned by a king) met to decide what to do about Scotland's throne. There were some supporters of the absent James (Jacobites) as well as a strong Williamite party. John Graham of Claverhouse, Viscount Dundee (1649-89) being one of the former, had taken up arms in support of James II.

The Duke of Gordon, Castle Governor, had been ordered by James to hold the Castle on his behalf. This he did half-heartedly against a blockading force which numbered 7,000. The defending garrison at the start of the siege numbered 160. Towards the end the number of effective manpower scarcely exceeded 40.

On 18 March 1689 Viscount Dundee, on his way out of Edinburgh with a group of 60 horse to organise a Jacobite army in the Highlands, paid a secret visit to Gordon at the western postern gate of the Castle, climbing up the steep Castle rock to get there. He is said to have tried to persuade him to leave the Castle in charge of his deputy and join Dundee's Jacobite clans in the north, but Gordon refused to leave and Dundee went north without him. Gordon had promised to hold out for 20 days at the end of which time Dundee hoped to be able to come to his relief with an army. Dundee however met his death at the Battle of Killiecrankie on 22 July.

In his *History of The Clan Macpherson,* entitled 'The Posterity of the Three Brethren', Alan G. Macpherson (my cousin!) writes of this siege:

> John Macpherson of the Killiehuntly family, and a 'very smart, ingen-
> ious, daring young man', had played a prominent part in the defence
> of the Castle during the Spring of 1689, acting as an envoy between
> the Duke of Gordon inside the Castle and the Jacobites outside. He
> repeatedly scaled the rocks to go back and forth in secret and avoid
> the Williamite government besiegers.

Figure 27. Plaque below the postern gate to mark the meeting pace between the
Viscount Dundee and the Duke of Gordon in 1689

A plaque at the postern gate overlooking St Cuthbert's churchyard marks the
meeting stating:

*At this postern John Graham of Claver House, Viscount Dundee held his
final conference with the Duke of Gordon, Governor of Edinburgh Castle,
on quitting the Convention of Estates – 18 March 1689.*

It is interesting to note that another plaque – an age weathered stone one –
exists on the south side of the Esplanade referring to the day following the
secret meeting between Dundee and Gordon. It reads:

*Hereabouts on 19 March 1689 David Leslie, Earl of Leven, raised a
Regiment of Foot in the space of two hours for the defence of the City. To
commemorate this act and also the gallant behaviour of the new Regiment
at the Battle of Killiecrankie some months later the City Magistrates con-
ferred upon Leven's Regiment the unique right of recruiting by beat of
drum in the City and the marching through the City at any time with
drums beating, colours flying and bayonets fixed.*

*The Regiment, later titled the 25th Edinburgh Regiment of Foot is now
known as the King's Own Scottish Borderers and frequently exercises the
privilege.*

(In modern times the soldiers of the KOSB march the length of Princes Street parading their colours to celebrate this honour.)

James, seeing that it was useless to resist further in the name of his cause, ordered Gordon to surrender. This he did on 14 June; he later made submission to William in London but afterwards served several terms of imprisonment on suspicion of Jacobite loyalties.

Thus ended the last of the great sieges upon the fortress, which, owing to its position, has never been taken by direct open assault in all of its stormy history apart from the two Scottish attacks on its ramparts by Sir Thomas Randolph, the first Earl of Moray, in 1312, and Sir William Douglas in 1341, which were really trick assaults.

Although not regarded as a 'siege' upon the fortress, the action in April 1916 of two German Zeppelin airships – cigar-shaped dirigibles inflated with gas – could have proved more serious had their 'bomb aimers' been more accurate. In all they dropped 47 bombs on Edinburgh, Leith and Colinton in the only air attack on a Scottish city in the First World War.

Edinburgh had no blackout, no air raid shelters, no ack-ack batteries and no fighter interceptors. It was a sitting target.

Edinburgh Castle was supposedly the magnet for the German bomb aimers – but it miraculously escaped damage. The reason for the 'miracle' lay in the fact that gunners at the Castle manned and fired the 1 o'clock gun

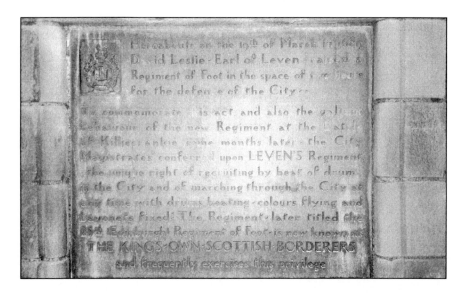

Figure 28. Plaque to David Leslie, Earl of Leven 1689 on the Esplanade

Figure 29. The postern gate high above the steep castle rock – meeting place between the Viscount Dundee and the Duke of Gordon

and chased the Zeppelin round the back of the Castle – unknown to the German airmen however only blank ammunition was available to the gunners!

Bombs probably weighing about 50lb each fell on the west side of the rock facing the present day Castle Terrace car park and in the Grassmarket, where no fewer than eleven fatalities occurred. It was a miracle that even more were not killed there in the packed closes of those days.

There is no memorial in the Grassmarket to those who died while the comparatively harmless explosion on the Castle Rock is marked by a plaque recording the long-forgotten event. This commemoration is placed high on the rock – and to climb up to it should not be attempted. (I did and my thighs were sore for two days afterwards!)

The plaque reads briefly:

On this spot a bomb fell during the German Air Raid
2nd April 1916.

Ancient legends abound about tunnels existing below the Castle, the favourite alleged to extend to Brown's Close in the Canongate and some say on down to Holyrood. Another is rumoured to run between Edinburgh and

Figure 30. Plaque very high on the rock to mark the position of a German Zepplin bomb raid during World War I – 1916

Craigmillar Castles. Had those who laid siege on the Castle known of the existence of such alleged tunnels then the course of history might have taken a different twist. Or might they have been the efforts of trying to escape?

In the 1980s a tunnel was constructed below the Castle to allow vehicular access – this was done by excavating through the Castle rock. In the process several skeletons were unearthed.

But today the only invaders besieging the Castle are the armies of tourists – who sadly for a period from 1999 missed out on the magnificent sight of kilted Scottish soldiers guarding the Castle in full Highland regalia when the latter were replaced, for the first time in living memory, by English troops! They were from the 1st Battalion Light Infantry recruited from the Durham area, kitted out in dark green trousers, clutching bugles!

CHAPTER FOUR

PRISONERS AND THE 'FRENCH CONNECTION'

The Castle's prisoners have been many and varied.

Thomas de Colville was the first State prisoner in 1210, innocently accused of plotting against William the Lion, grandson of David I.

In 1479 James III was suspicious of his younger brother Alexander Stewart, Duke of Albany, collaborating with the English to claim his crown. He therefore kept him imprisoned in David's Tower while he lived in the adjacent Royal apartments. But Albany escaped after luring his guards into his chamber to drink wine before a blazing fire, killing them when they became drowsy and roasting them in full armour on the fire. He escaped by rope over the rock. Ironically, before long James III was imprisoned for two months in David's Tower to be released by the intervention of Albany.

In 1516 Bishop and poet Gavin Douglas was accused of having received bulls from the Pope and was held captive. Later that year the third Lord Home was accused of dereliction of duty at Flodden. He, along with his brother, escaped from captivity but they were recaptured and subjected to barbaric punishment. Beheaded soon afterwards, their heads were displayed on the Tolbooth where they remained for all to see until 1521.

In 1540 James V heard that his companion of earlier years, Sir James Hamilton of Finnart, cupbearer, steward of the Royal household and architect for Royal palaces and castles, had as far back as 1528 contrived to murder the King in his bed at Holyroodhouse. He was convicted of high treason and executed.

In 1559 Mary of Lorraine ordered the detention of Sir John Maxwell, fourth Lord Herries, for heresy. He escaped by lowering himself over the Castle wall with the aid of a rope, was later recaptured and remained in the Castle until freed by Sir William Kirkcaldy.

James VI met with an adversary in 1584 in the person of Francis, fifth Earl of Bothwell, one of the most reckless and peace-destroying men of his time. Amongst other charges he was apprehended for conspiring with witches in an attempt to drown the King. He escaped and later attempted to seize the King and his Queen in Holyroodhouse. A reward was offered for his assassination; the King personally took part in a hunt for him but he remained at large.

The same James VI (and I of England) did not appear to be popular for another thorn in his flesh, Patrick Stewart, second Earl of Orkney, was imprisoned in 1609 for inciting rebellion in that county. Released on sureties he was again remanded for further misbehaviour and eventually beheaded at the Cross of Edinburgh.

Many prisoners of the 1745 Jacobite rebellion were held in the Castle.

The vaults have been put to a number of uses from an arsenal and barracks to a bakehouse but they are best remembered between 1757 and 1811 for accommodating as many as a thousand prisoners of war, in particular, soldiers captured during the Napoleonic wars with France in the eighteenth and nineteenth centuries – the 'French Connection'. Still in existence are some of the graffiti scrawled by them in the stonework of the entrance door. A number of the surviving pieces of handicraft which they made and sold to make money can be seen in the National War Museum of Scotland.

In addition to the French prisoners were Spanish, German, Dutch, Irish and American. Most were sailors who slept in hammocks suspended from the walls.

The Scottish slang word 'clink' for jail or prison is believed to have originated in these prison vaults owing to the chains which were used to fasten the doors – the slightest movement made them 'clink'.

Of all the prisoners held in the Castle the most famous are probably the Marquis of Argyll and his son the ninth Earl of Argyll.

In 1661 the father, accused of supporting Cromwell, was led from this thick walled prison, known then as Constable's Tower and afterwards as the **Argyle Tower** (the 'family prison') – now the upper storeys of the **Portcullis Gate**.[5] He was executed at the Mercat Cross and his head later fixed above the Tolbooth.

Twenty years later his son was arrested for treason and held within the 15 ft thick walls of the same prison. Found guilty and condemned to death – a sentence which was confirmed by King Charles II – he determined to escape. His step-daughter, accompanied by a page, was granted permission to bid her last farewells to him. The epic is well known of how Argyll exchanged clothes with the page and escorted his step-daughter through the Castle gates to his freedom in Holland for four years. He returned, after that time, to head a National uprising in support of Monmouth's rebellion

[5] **Portcullis Gate** (1574-7) was built after the long siege of 1568-73 on the main gateway into the Castle. It stands on the site of the Medieval Constable's Tower. The top storey was added in 1887.

Figure 31. Portcullis Gateway and Argyle Tower

against King James II (of England) in 1685. This failed and Argyll was captured once again and placed in the Argyle Tower – this time in iron fetters. After sentence he was led, calmly, to the Mercat Cross where he was beheaded, as his father was, and his head placed on the Tolbooth gable (See Chapter 5.)

Overlooking the New Town quite near the Argyle Tower, although not linked historically with it, stands the **Argyle Battery** (or Six Gun Battery), named after the second Duke of Argyll, C-in-C Scotland in 1715.

In 1779 the men of the Argyll Fencibles – stationed in the Castle – refused to wear the government-issue sporrans and cartridge boxes. These men were Campbells

Many had joined up believing they would be able to wear Highland dress in the army. To them this included the traditional deerskin sporran, shot-bag and powder horn of their ancestors. Rather than listen to their grievances the government chose to regard their refusal as mutiny. The mutineers were to be made an example of. First they had to be enticed out of the Castle where they could not be attacked without huge loss of life and a ploy was devised: Lord Frederick Campbell – someone the Campbells trusted – ordered them to parade on Leith Links for field exercises. No mention was made of the hated equipment. When they arrived they found the Dragoons waiting. Three wagons rolled up and the sporrans and cartridge-boxes were unloaded. The men were ordered to collect their equipment. They refused. As an example four were picked out and flogged in full view of the others.

The sick and convalescing had been left in the Castle while the others paraded on Leith Links. When news of the floggings reached them the authorities really did have a mutiny on their hands. Incensed by the deception the sick inmates raised the drawbridge as an act of protest and took possession of the fortress. However a few sick men could not hope to hold a whole Castle. When the Dragoons arrived they attacked the building, swarmed over its gates and took the inmates prisoner.

Two men were tried and found guilty of mutiny; both were sentenced to several years' foreign service. What had started out as a protest against substandard equipment had escalated into a full-blown mutiny in which the Castle had been briefly held.

The Highlanders paid a high price for their stand. Two were sent into exile while another four had the skin flayed off their backs with fierce floggings. In trying to hold onto their culture they had come up against the ignorance and prejudice of the British army.

To bring us further 'up-to-date', if we can call it that, there is behind **Dury's Battery** a small Military Prison built about 1842. It was designed to house offenders from all Scottish garrisons, not only from the Castle, and to provide solitary confinement for all its inmates. Let us look at the sentence of one offender:

In July 1844 Private Robert Ewing of the 26th Cameronian Regiment was caught drunk on guard duty while stationed in the Castle. This was a serious offence. He was sentenced to 2 months solitary confinement. His punishment included separating strands of old tarred rope, or oakum, for reuse, stone breaking and yard cleaning. The prison block illustrates the type of cell in use at the time with a model of Ewing sitting separating strands of tarred rope. He was aged 24 from Bonhill in Dunbartonshire, and when caught had been in the Army for four years. During the remainder of his 21 years service he served in the East Indies, China and Bermuda and earned good conduct pay and badges.

(By a strange coincidence my late mother-in-law's maiden name was Ewing and she hailed from the same area as Private Ewing mentioned on page 44 and my late wife had a cousin of the same name as the Private! We are not aware, however, of any family connection but who knows?)

The Prison was last used in 1923.

In 2004 following a £3.5 million revamp the public was given a rare glimpse into the life of an eighteenth century prisoner of war. Visitors are able to go back in time to experience the sights, sounds and smells of the castle vaults when crammed with prisoners in 1781.

The new permanent attraction in the depths of the castle recreates minute details of the daily lives of hundreds of captured sailors. Authentic prison clothes dangle between hammocks as animated shadows move across the walls and prisoners' voices of different nationalities echo round the rooms. Puddles have even been created on the cobbles to authenticate the journey back in time while the smell changes as visitors move through the vaults. As mentioned earlier in this chapter graffiti had been found in the vaults, some of it over two hundred years old. Wood has been carved with political messages and pictures including a gallows dangling the then Prime Minister, Lord North.

More than a hundred Frenchmen, many suffering from scurvy, were seized in the West Indies and held in the vaults as were a party of Americans from the privateer *Newfoundland* which included two crewmen of the founder of the American navy – Kirkcudbright-born John Paul Jones. Many of the inmates were considered to be pirates or rebels and they suffered many months of incarceration.

A visit to the vaults will enable people to see how prisoners were treated in bygone days and the conditions in which they were kept long before the introduction of the terms of the Geneva Convention!

CHAPTER FIVE

A DISCOVERY – ON REFLECTION

At this stage I would like to introduce the reader to a few interesting extracts from a very old book which I discovered in a second-hand bookshop in the village of West Linton after I had completed my research. The book is a heavy leather-bound tome entitled *The Story of Edinburgh Castle*, published by George G. Harrop & Co. in 1913 and written by Louis Weirter with an introduction by Prof. Sir Patrick Geddes ('Edinburgh's greatest all-round citizen') and includes many relevant and beautiful sketches – a book worthy, in my estimation, of re-issue at some future date (in paperback of course!)

I feel the following adds extra 'colour' to my research:

1093 – On hearing of the death of his brother Malcolm on the battlefield, Donald Bane proclaimed himself King, and at the head of an army of wild Highlanders from the west marched on Edinburgh. His immediate object was to take the life of Edgar, the youthful heir to the throne, while the Court and family, then lodged within the Castle walls, were mourning their triple loss. Relying on the almost inaccessible rock to hold his prey, Donald Bane, 'The Fair-headed', determined to secure the regular access facing the town from the east side. But fate was against him. Through a postern on the west side, down a steep declivity of the rock, the children escaped and through it a few days later the body of Margaret was secretly conveyed and taken to Dunfermline Abbey. There is a legend to the effect that, during the escape, a miraculous mist arose from the sea which veiled the cortege from the view of the insurgents, and covered it for a distance of nine miles until it had crossed the Forth.

Margaret was canonized by Pope Innocent IV in 1250, and at the Reformation the Abbot removed her head bearing 'the flowing auburn hair' in a jewelled casket, and fled with it to the Castle. Just before the birth of her son James, Mary Queen of Scots had the head of Queen Margaret brought to her at the Castle, in order that she might receive benefit from the presence of the sacred relic. After her enforced flight the relic remained for some time in safe custody in Scotland; it was afterwards taken successively to Antwerp and to the Jesuit College at Douai, and in the French Revolution it disappeared.

1617 – James VI of Scotland and I of England had an interesting personality, and his quaint figure was missed from the walks of the Castle; he looked very stout from the peculiar fashion of his doublet, which was quilted, so as to be stiletto-proof; he walked clumsily, owing to the weakness of his legs, which never seemed to have strength enough to support his body. He kept his heavy eyes continually rolling, and his tongue when he spoke seemed to be too large for his mouth; his utterance was in consequence thick and indistinct. 'Dirty in his habits, he never washed his hands but simply wiped the points of his fingers with a wet napkin. He always fiddled about with his fingers, and as he walked he was often leaning on other men's shoulders.' So if this picture be correct, James certainly did not inherit any of the elegance ascribed to his mother (Mary Queen of Scots).

1650 – 'In a rare old extract of 1650 the appearance is recorded of a horrible apparition, which created great alarm in the fortress. On a dark and gloomy night the sentinel, under the shadow of the gloomy half-moon, was alarmed by the beating of a drum upon the Esplanade and the tread of marching feet, on which he fired his musket. Colonel Dundas hurried forth, but could see nothing on the bleak expanse, the site of the now demolished Spur. The sentinel was truncheoned and another put in his place, to whom the same thing happened, and he too fired his musket, affirming that he heard the tread of soldiers marching to the tuck of drums. To Dundas nothing was visible, nothing audible but the moan of an autumn wind. He took a musket and the post of the sentinel. Anon he heard the old Scots march beaten by an invisible drummer, who came close up to the gate – then came other sounds – the tramp of many feet and clank of accoutrements; still nothing was visible, 'til the whole impalpable array seemed to halt close by Dundas (the Governor), who was bewildered with consternation. Again the drum was heard beating the English march, and then the French march, when the alarm was sounded; but the next drums that were beaten there were those of Oliver Cromwell.'

1681 – In 1681 the new Marquis of Argyll was committed a third time to the Castle for refusing to take the oath required by the Test Act as Commissioner of the Scottish Treasury, and on 12 December, being found guilty of 'treason and leasing telling', he was sentenced to death. Precautions were taken to prevent rioting; the guards of the Castle were strengthened, and extra patrols were mounted in the City. Argyll, like his father, had decided on a plan of escape with the assistance of his daughter-in-law, the Lady Sophia Lindsay, of Balcarres. The story goes that she with her page paid a visit to the State prison with the object of bidding him a last farewell.

Exchanging his own costume for that of her attendant, he sallied forth from his own cell bearing her train aloft from the dirty paving slabs, which were wet with slush of a previous snowstorm. He successfully managed to evade his guards until the couple reached the outer gate, when he was challenged by the sentry on guard, which made him forget his duty of train-bearer, whereby the silken robes of the Lady Lindsay were allowed to drop in the mud. With wonderful presence of mind his companion lifted her bedraggled train and threw it across the face of her seeming attendant with the exclamation, 'Thou careless loon!' The sentry, highly amused at the punishment, and at the dirty face of Argyll, allowed them to pass. Lady Lindsay entered her coach, the Earl got behind a flunkey, and they rapidly drove away out of sight of the Castle, and the Earl was able to make good his escape to Holland. As for Lady Lindsay, she was arrested when the authorities discovered what had transpired, and was confined in the Tolbooth.

(Shades of *The Scarlet Pimpernel* or the deeds of Douglas Fairbanks Jr, or Errol Flynn?)

CHAPTER SIX

THE 'JACOBITE CONNECTION'

The Castle has had its connection with the Jacobites too – during the 1715 and the 1745 Rebellions (known as the '15 and '45 Rebellions).

Within days of George I (the 'Wee German Lairdie') coming to the throne in 1714 the Commander of the Castle received orders to fortify the garrison against a possible Jacobite rising. A year later a large Jacobite army, headed by the Earl of Mar, had its eye on the most prized and important stronghold in Scotland.

One dark night (8 September 1715) a few chosen men were given the task of scaling the Castle wall. They were to be assisted from within – a rope ladder being dropped to speed their ascent. Owing to some 'careless talk' by one of Mar's own men, however, the plan was made known to the Castle's Deputy Governor who chose, at first, to ignore the warning. The unsuspecting Jacobites handled the affair badly – the ascending party was late in turning up; the ladder was too short; and in the Castle above a change of watch took place. Meanwhile the Deputy Governor had had second thoughts on the matter and advised the Officer of the Guard of the impending attack.

Sentries were doubled and one of them fired a shot to raise the alarm after the attacking party had climbed a good length up the rock face. In their hasty descent they left behind four wounded men who were taken prisoner. The traitor within the Castle, Sergeant William Ainslie, was hanged over the postern wall as a warning to those below.

It is not known whether or not it is a 'throwback' to those days of the '15 Rebellion but a length of rope is today held at the Central Fire Station in Edinburgh specially for the purpose of rescuing, from above, anyone foolish enough to climb and become trapped on any of the sheer faces of the Castle Rock. No doubt, unlike that used by the Jacobites, the rope is of a suitable length to reach the ground below!

On one occasion in 1995 a climber was plucked to safety by fire officers after trying to scale the Castle Rock. The rescue operation cost £800 to carry out and tied up sixteen fire-fighters from a specialised crew for an hour. One fire-fighter abseiled down the Castle wall to reach the man who was then placed on a turntable ladder, which pulled him down from the rock face.

The rescue operation involved two pumping appliances, an emergency tender and a turntable ladder. A fire spokesman said resources are provided in the Brigade's budget and cannot be recouped, and he added, 'Operations like this take up resources of the brigade that could be used for proper emergencies.' The man was later charged with a breach of the peace.

While on the subject it may be of interest to know that in Lothian and Borders Fire Brigade Museum at Lauriston are two 'cleiks' measuring 30 ft long and weighing ¾ hundredweight. Believed to date from the early 1400s they were said to have been used in the Castle for pulling burning thatch from buildings.

In 1745, when the Highlanders of Bonnie Prince Charlie, grandson of James VII, were in possession of the city, the Deputy Governor ordered the Castle guns to open fire upon the' town below. Bombardment was maintained for two days – considerable havoc was wrought and no end of alarm caused to the peaceful citizens of the community.

To this day it is said that a relic of that bombardment – a cannonball – may be seen embedded in the wall of a building in Castle Hill, which, for obvious reasons, is known as 'Cannonball House'. An alternative and more logical explanation for its existence is that it was to mark the gravitation height of Edinburgh's first piped water supply in 1681.

In 1746 a number of 'tronemen' assisted the hangman to carry the captured banners of Prince Charlie from the Castle to the Mercat Cross for public burning. In those days 'tronemen' were the equivalent of modern chimney sweeps earning their title after their place of gathering at the public weighbeam opposite the Tron Church where they were paid money for the soot which they had collected and weighed. They were affectionately referred to as the 'Custodians of the Flues', twelve of whom were daily elected to 'call the streets' seeking business and keeping a watchful eye out for fires within the Old Town. For this duty they were paid the princely sum of 5s. (25p) per annum! They wore a uniform of frock coat with full skirt, short apron, knee breeches and buckled shoes and reserved the right to flaunt a broad bonnet.

The Highlanders, needless to say, did not capture the Castle and its long military history as a fortification thus came to a close.

During the aftermath of the Jacobite Rising of 1745 a Cart Shed was built in 1746 to hold fifty provision carts to supply the large garrison of Redcoats in the Castle. The Cart Shed is now used as a Restaurant offering self and table service.

CHAPTER SEVEN

THE CASTLE GOVERNORS

The history of Edinburgh Castle is particularly bloody and the Governor always had to ensure that it was well fortified and kept out of enemy hands.

Over the centuries there have been many governors, including some of the following:

- Galfrid de Melville of Melville in Lothian was appointed Governor in 1153.

- In 1278 Governor William of Kinghorn gave up the Castle to the Plantagenet King Edward I.

- Sir Radulph Basset de Drayton was appointed Governor by Edward I in 1291 and took over the Castle after just 15 days of siege.

- He was succeeded by Walter de Huntercombe, Baron of Northumberland, in 1296, but the next year William Wallace recaptured the Castle for Scotland.

- The Governor didn't always have to be Scottish, however – in 1304 Sir Piers de Lombard, a brave knight of Gascony, got the job.

- During the reign of David I the Castle became so well fortified that with a proper garrison the Duke of Rothesay was able to resist the attacking efforts of Henry IV in 1400.

- Sir William Crichton was Governor in 1438 and in 1566 Sir James Balfour of Pittendreich was 'Keeper' of the Castle for Mary Queen of Scots.

- Probably the most famous of the long line of Governors was Sir William Kirkcaldy of Grange as already mentioned in a previous chapter. On behalf of his Queen he carried out a 5 year long defence of the Castle against overwhelming odds. This ended in 1573.

- In 1574 George Douglas of Parkhead was in post.

- In rapid succession the following were appointed – Walter Dundas 1650, Colonel Newman 1658 and the Earl of Middleton 1661.

- In 1686 James II appointed the first Duke of Gordon and Lt Colonel Stuart was Deputy in 1715.

- In the year 1745 Generals Guest and Preston were both appointed.

The tradition of the General Officer Commanding the Army in Scotland automatically becoming Governor began on 11 February 1936, when Parliament was informed that the ancient title of Governor was to be revived. Previously the post had been out of use since 1860 and before that the holders were known as Constables, Wardens or

Figure 32. The Governor's House

Keepers, and were expected to defend the Castle to the last man when under siege.

The GOC has little to do with the day-to-day running of Scotland's top tourist attraction. Instead, the majority of duties is left to the Castle garrison commander and the owners, Historic Scotland.[6]

The GOC has no powers 'to cut anyone's head off' or close the Castle gates. It is really an honorary appointment. In the commission which is signed on behalf of the Queen by the Secretary of State for Scotland, it even says 'without any duties or powers'.

The Governor's House, a 'pleasing restrained classical building' was built in 1742. On each side are wings built originally to house the Master Gunner and Storekeeper. The right wing is still the residence of the Governor, while the rest of the house is used as the Officers' Mess of the Castle garrison.

The 122nd Governor, Major General Jonathan Hall, was appointed in July 1995 replacing General Mike Scott, a Falklands war hero, and in 1998 Major General Mark Strudwick took up his post as 123rd Governor, followed by Major General Robert Gordon in May 2000 and Major General Euan Loudon in July 2004.

---

[6] **Historic Scotland** safeguards the Nation's built heritage and promotes its understanding and enjoyment. Over 300 monuments and properties are maintained and it is the country's largest operator of visitor attractions. Scotland has a wealth of prehistoric sites and historic buildings and Historic Scotland has a team of archaeologists, historians, conservators, architects, technical staff, draughtsmen and managers to care for them. There are over 40,000 protected buildings etc.

CHAPTER EIGHT

MACHINERY OF WAR

Machines of war, guns both ancient and modern, celebrate the Castle's military might. Cannon line the battlements, with their portholes framing magnificent views of the City. These include the **Argyle Battery** or Six Gun Battery to the right of the **Portcullis Gate** built in the 1730s; **Mills Mount Battery** beyond the Argyle looking out to the north; **Dury's Battery** named after Theodore Dury who rebuilt the Castle's northern walls in the early eighteenth century and the **Half Moon** and **Forewall Batteries** guarding the south-east and east battlements respectively.

Ancient pistols illustrate past battles in the museums, housed in former barrack blocks and the hospital, which are devoted to the history of the Scottish Regiments (See Chapter 12.)

Under the hammerbeam roof of the **Great Hall**[7] built for James IV and the meeting place of the Scottish Parliament until the mid-seventeenth century when Charles I ordained that a splendid new hall be built behind St Giles Cathedral, tiny mortar cannons line the walls.

Only one of the Castle's many guns is regularly fired, the **one o'clock** time signal which booms out across the City every day except Sunday. The history behind this gun begins in 1853.

On a visit to Edinburgh a foreign sea captain went home and reported that no-one in Edinburgh could tell him the current time of day. The citizens of Edinburgh took this to heart and in 1853 Professor Piazzi Smyth, the Astronomer Royal for Scotland, arranged for a time signal in the form of a large ball to be erected on the top of Nelson's Monument on Calton Hill. Just before 1 o'clock each day it would be hoisted to the top of the mast and

---

[7] The **Great Hall** (1503-13). Built for James IV (1488-1513) as a majestic setting for ceremonial occasions it was converted into a soldiers' barrack by Cromwell. Restored in 1887 (and to its present state in 1891) it is used today for State and Royal functions. Only the great hammerbeam roof is medieval. The wall-panelling, stained glass windows and fireplace are Victorian. The arms and armour are on loan from the armouries of the Tower of London. The wall decorations include Coats of Arms, lions, roses, thistles and lilies and the heraldic stained glass plays its part in relating Scotland's history. One gun on prominent display is the King Charles II Cannon, a field gun cast in bronze in Rotterdam by John Ouderogge, intended to fire 4 pound round shot. It may be the sole survivor from an order placed with the Dutchman in 1675 by Robert Mylne, Provost of Linlithgow. An exceptionally fine piece of artillery, it is also a rare survival of a gun made for the Kings of Scotland. Engraved on the barrel are the Royal Arms of Scotland.

Figure 33. Part of the Argyle Battery

exactly at one o'clock it was lowered. At sea, ships' captains on the Firth of Forth could spot this signal through their telescopes and set their chronometers accurately.

But since it was of no use in fog or bad visibility a more accurate check was required and in 1861 a 4,200 ft long copper wire was fixed between the Royal Observatory on the Calton Hill and Edinburgh Castle; a shorter wire stretched from the Royal Observatory to Nelson's Monument. An electric clock was connected to the wire and hung on the wall near the Half Moon Battery in the Castle. The time of 1 o'clock was decided upon just as it was at Greenwich near London.

As the second hand on the clock reached 1 o'clock a piece of machinery triggered off the gun which was only loaded with gunpowder. Pigeons flew off the Castle ramparts as they do today and people set their watches to the correct time. Although they know it happens daily Edinburgh citizens never fail to jump as the gun goes off as also visitors to the capital do in wonder.

For obvious reasons the gun was not fired during World Wars I and II.

In 1965 the gun (then a World War II Howitzer) came under fire from angry civil servants. Army gunners had stepped up the power of the cannon charge and as a result, smashed windows and light bulbs in parts of the Castle round the Half Moon Battery, knocked over exhibits in the Castle Museum

Figure 34. Part of Dury's Battery

Figure 35. A display of armour and weaponry in the Great Hall

Figure 36. The one o'clock gun booms across the City every week-day

and blew slates off the guardhouse roof. Masonry around the Battery was also damaged by vibrations caused by the firing of both the one o'clock gun and Ceremonial 21 gun salutes for Royal birthdays.

The situation led to an angry exchange of letters between the Army's Scottish Command, the (then) Ministry of Works and the War Office. Caught up in the 'crossfire' were residents in the exclusive Ramsay Garden flats next to the Castle Esplanade. They claimed their ceilings were damaged by vibrations because they were in the direct line of fire of the blank charges.

After a three month battle of words senior officers at Scottish Command finally gave in and cut back the charge.

In the early 1970s a bomb left in a compartment beside the ruined David's Tower exploded during a performance of the Military Tattoo. Fortunately no-one was injured. The explosion, however, caused considerable damage to the surrounding masonry, including weakening the gun platform of the Half Moon Battery so badly that all future gun salutes and the one o'clock gun were to be fired from the Mills Mount Battery facing Princes Street. In 2001 the 25lb howitzer, introduced in 1952, became increasingly difficult to maintain and was replaced with a 105 mm light gun.

It is very unlikely that there is a 1 o'clock gun fired anywhere else in the UK. There are a number of 12 o'clock firings on the Continent but apparently Edinburgh chose a 1 o'clock firing as being more economical!

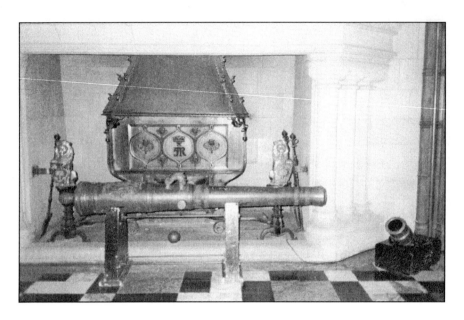

Figure 37. King Charles II cannon in the Great Hall

The regular stewards at the Castle are often asked strange questions – one such was 'At what time does the 1 o'clock gun go off?' to which the steward tactfully replied, 'At 12.60 Scottish time!'

The Castle's most famous cannon is **Mons Meg** of the type known as 'bombard', regarded as a kind of Scottish palladium. She is a huge piece of antique artillery made of long iron bars hooped together, weighing nearly 6 tons, 13 ft long and measuring 2 ft within the bore.

There are various stories as to her origin: one tradition, and the most likely one, asserts that she was made in the 1440s at Mons in Hainault, Belgium, and sent as a gift, at a cost of £1,536, from the Duke of Burgundy to his nephew by marriage, James II, in 1457. Another says that she was forged in Edinburgh Castle and a third that she was forged at Castle Douglas in Galloway by a blacksmith named McKim who presented her to James II at the siege of Threave Castle in 1455. He received in return the lands of Mollance (locally pronounced Monce or Mons) whence the name 'Mollance Meg' after his wife, and later corrupted to Mons Meg.

She was employed at the siege of Dumbarton in 1488 and of Norham Castle in 1497 and the 'great iron murderer called Muckle Meg' was among the captured guns listed by Cromwell as taken in Edinburgh Castle in 1650.

Mons Meg is referred to in Scott's 'Bonnie Dundee' but by that time she

Figure 38. "Mons Meg"

was incapable of speaking even 'twa words or three' for while firing a Royal salute in 1680 to the Duke of York (afterwards James VII and II of England), Charles II's brother, she burst her barrel thus rendering her useless and abandoned.

Having been in the Tower of London between 1754 and 1829 she was returned to Edinburgh in 1829 at Sir Walter Scott's request, and to the joy of the Scottish people.

She was on display near St Margaret's Chapel until the weather was affecting the metal and for twenty years she resided sheltered from the elements in the Castle vaults; however in 2001 she took up an honoured position near St Margaret's Chapel after having been given a sophisticated coating to enable her to withstand the weather conditions.

In the 1890s she had an ornate gun carriage dating back to the fifteenth century. In 1934 this was restored to its original design in Scottish oak at the expense of Lord Provost Sir William Thomson. In 1985 she travelled to Halstead in Kent for examination by experts from the Tower of London. They wanted to establish her weight and to examine the barrel by x-ray. This mighty almost 6-ton siege gun which once took a hundred men and many oxen to move, and served in scores of Scottish battles with an impressive range of over two miles, is now a much photographed item by visitors. She was truly the 'Trident Submarine' of her day!

Now the only martial displays to be seen in the Castle are when the troops march on the Esplanade to the strains of the bagpipes during the Military Tattoo every August.

CHAPTER NINE

THE CASTLE'S 'SECURE LOCH'

In medieval days a castle for added protection was not complete without a moat and Edinburgh Castle was no exception. A small moat did front the Castle in the sixteenth century, protecting it from attack from the Esplanade area – a drill hall and Tattoo storehouse were built over it in the nineteenth century.

The 'moat' we are about to research however did not surround the Castle walls but took the form of a man-made loch which for over three centuries submerged what is now Princes Street Gardens on the north side of the Castle cliffs and was appropriately called the **Nor' Loch**.

Back in early medieval times there was a Royal pleasure garden beneath the Castle Rock, a place where knights jousted in the joyous pageantry of the tournament. But James II[8] did not feel as secure as his predecessors and had the garden flooded and a loch formed from the base of the rock to Netherbow Port. With the loch controlled by a dam and sluice, James added further security in the form of a wall and within it was the **Wellhouse Tower**. Legend carries this tower back to the days of St Margaret, and the Edinburgh councillors took great pains to ensure its state of repair.

Once they had the loch the people of Edinburgh did not seem sure what to do with it – a boating loch that fleshers and butchers were ordered to use as a dump; a barrier which smugglers crossed to avoid Customs dues, their goods having been landed at the Drum Sands or Figgate Whins and taken through the farmland of what is now North Edinburgh. There are tales of secret passages from the lochside to the centre of Edinburgh, of mysterious men labouring into Lady Stair's or Advocates Closes with bundles of contraband.

But the City Fathers had other ideas about the loch – why not duck people in it! Not just anybody – but adulterers, dishonest merchants, blasphemers and the like.

While women were ducked at the stool – a crude see-saw construction with a rough seat strapped to one end – two merchants who were caught

[8] **James II** was nicknamed 'James of the Fiery Face' because of a large birthmark on his face.

tampering with their weights were tossed into the loch at the end of a rope and dragged to and fro by a lynch mob. That was 1609.

A bit more sinister was the fate in 1628 of a brother and two sisters named Sinclair; he was convicted of having committed incest with both and a sentence of drowning was administered to all three. They were shut into a chest which was then holed and thrown into the loch.

In 1635 a Lawnmarket hawker, Betty Trot, was accused of theft and condemned to be ducked four times. She waited until she was at the ducking stool, however, before she rebelled. First she knocked the hangman – who was about to tie her to the stool – into the loch then she ran for a boat and rowed away. Two boatloads of city officials gave chase but Betty rocked her craft to fend them off. Some of her pursuers fell into the water to the delight of the watching crowd but Betty was outmanoeuvred. She put up her hands to surrender, her boat was boarded by a handful of officers, and she capsized the lot of them into the loch! Betty was ducked after all – but with company.

In 1663 a woman drowned while being ducked and the Scots Estates Parliament was horrified. Ducking was banned and only twenty years later the ducking stool was removed.

In spite of such inhumanity, the Estates did nothing to prevent witches from being thrown into the loch with toes and thumbs tied together. If a witch floated she was guilty and could be burned on the Castle Hill. If, however, she sank she was innocent and could be set free – provided she had

Figure 39. The Castle from the Scott Monument showing Princes Street Gardens (the site of the Nor' Loch), the Royal Scottish Art Gallery and the National Gallery of Scotland

Figure 40. Ruin of the ancient Wellhouse Tower

not drowned! Of the 150 odd people who drowned in the loch, most were suicides.

To 'tak a dook at the pot' was an old Edinburgh phrase for attempting suicide, and the Pot in question was a 15 ft deep pool roughly where the old GPO was situated, opposite Register House in the East End of Princes Street.

In 1707, possibly to celebrate the Union of Parliaments, a Robert Balfour, Master of Burleigh, murdered a teacher from Inverkeithing. He was sentenced to be hanged at Edinburgh Cross in January 1710, but he escaped and dived into the loch – braving the eels, rats and floating sewage. He did not emerge from the Pot but later it was discovered that he had swum to the north shore and escaped.

Another escaper was a woman of the same century. After leaping into the Pot, she discovered that her wide, hooped skirt was acting as a lifebelt; filled with air, it kept her afloat – and then the wind caught her. Screaming for help she was whisked across the loch and a boat was rowed to her aid but too late ... the wind had blown her clear across to Lochside Farm on the opposite shore.

Boggy land separated the Castle from Princes Street and the earthen **Mound** bisected where the loch had once been. By 1787 as it was serving no useful purpose and becoming stagnant the Town Council ordered it to be drained with all possible speed. By 1821 the portion in the west had been

Figure 41. St Margaret's Well at the base of the Castle Rock

converted into a pleasure ground, but the portion in the east remained a reedy marshy ground. No more would the Cowgate Taverns sell Nor' Loch trout or eel pie, and now footpads waited for the unwary where scolding wives had once been ducked.

Today the ruin of the **Wellhouse Tower** stands at the base of the Castle Rock on the south side of the railway line skirting Princes Street Gardens and marked by the following inscription:

St Margaret's Well

The fountain of the Ancient Wellhouse Tower celebrated in the history of the Castle since the time of St Margaret, Queen of Scotland in the 11th century. It was restored by the Officers of the 93rd Sutherland Highlanders in 1873.

Immediately above it on top of the crag stood a bastion on which a crane was used in bringing up the water from the Wellhouse. An elaborate scheme for a hand-chain pump in two stages was contemplated in the eighteenth century but was never carried into effect.

The only water left is now in the ornate **Fountain** in the shadow of St Cuthbert's Kirk.

Figure 42. Ross Fountain in Princes Street Gardens

But as for Princes Street Gardens, once described as a filthy and offensive bog, and now recognised as the jewel in the crown of the City's parks, very few know that the west part is still privately owned – by the Queen! The freedom of the gardens is thanks to the generosity of the Crown.

King William IV was on the throne when the decision was taken to release the west gardens for public use – the former Nor' Loch. For an annual rent of £32 the City of Edinburgh took over the area for cattle grazing.

The land was later taken over by the Princes Street Proprietors, the well-to-do living opposite the gardens. They drained the land and laid it out in a series of walks – creating the most exclusive gardens in the City. But plans for a railway line in the 1830s outraged them and they gained permission to erect a parapet and railings around the land, sealing it entirely from the public.

It wasn't until 1876, when Princes Street became commercialised, that the gardens were finally handed over to the old Edinburgh Corporation and opened fully to the public. They continue to thrive and prosper, providing the people of Edinburgh and the many visitors from around the globe with a wonderful setting for relaxation and enjoyment ... but no longer a 'secure defence for the fortress'!

CHAPTER TEN

EDINBURGH – 'THE REAL JERUSALEM' – 'THE BIBLE CONNECTION'

In this chapter let us digress for a short while from our main topic of Edinburgh Castle to look at an unexplained coincidence in comparing Edinburgh, in which the Castle plays a prominent part, with Jerusalem.

The description is reproduced here with the kind permission of the magazine *Scottish Memories*:

Edinburgh has had many descriptions applied to it in its long and turbulent history but surely the strangest is the claim that Scotland's capital and the Biblical Jerusalem are one and the same place!

The claim was made in *Britain, the Key to World History* written over 50 years ago by Comyns Beaumont, a journalist. Israel's Jerusalem, he says, in no way corresponds to descriptions of the city which appear in the Bible or in the works of Josephus, the Jewish historian of Roman times.

But according to Beaumont, the geography of Edinburgh tallies exactly with the old accounts of the Holy City. Edinburgh Castle fits the Biblical description of Zion and the Citadel, and the Castle moat evidently solves a problem which has puzzled scholars for years. According to 2 Samuel, 'David dwelt in the fort and called it the City of David. And David built round about from Millo onwards.'

Experts have never conclusively worked out where Millo was in Jerusalem. But Beaumont is confident that it's the moat which protected the Castle from attack from the Esplanade.

The Esplanade itself corresponds to Mount Opel and the Upper City of Jerusalem while at the head of the High Street the Lawnmarket marks the site of Upper Market Place. The ravine now partly filled in and spanned by George IV Bridge is the Tyropoean Valley of Biblical times, which was dominated by the great Tower of Antonia, built by Herod to guard the Temple. Hadrian ordered the tower to be razed and Beaumont claims that the great heaps of debris which formed the foundations for Edinburgh's Mound – linking Princes Street to the High Street – were the long forgotten remains of the Antonia.

Next come Bezetha and the Pool of Bethesda. Bezetha was a 'new town' built across the Valley of Jehosophat and the Pool of Bethesda from the Holy City to accommodate the overflow from Jerusalem's expanding population.

Beaumont points to the foot of the Calton Hill and the site of Princes Street as Bezetha. Between them and the Old Town lies the valley now occupied by Waverley Station and Princes Street Gardens – all that remains of the Nor' Loch, drained when Edinburgh's New Town was built.

Not all of Beaumont's proofs are in the city centre. He suggests that Arthur's Seat – the extinct volcano that looms to the south-east of Princes Street – is the exact position where the Mount of Olives should be. And Holyrood House, which sits at its base, corresponds to King Solomon's cedar palace – the House of the Forest of Lebanon.

The author sees Joppa as easy justification for his theory. Jerusalem's port has that name, and Edinburgh, too, has its Joppa by the sea. Beaumont concludes his case by identifying Corstorphine Hill with the Biblical Mount Tophet – the Place of Burning – and the Gogar district with Golgotha. The Place of Skulls where Christ was crucified is not in Israel, he claims, but four miles from the Centre of Edinburgh.

Beaumont claims that there was a vast conspiracy to place the scene of Old Israel's history thousands of miles from where they actually happened in Scotland's Capital.

The reader, or visitor, is left to make his or her own judgement of this strange supposition!

CHAPTER ELEVEN

THE CASTLE IN A MODERN ROLE

During the days of the annual Edinburgh International Festival the Castle plays an important role. Not only does it sit in grandeur during the day overlooking the majestic ceremonies being performed below it in the City and hailed as Edinburgh's most photographed and Scotland's most visited 'citizen', but it also enjoys taking part in the festivities. The Castle buildings comprise a massive structure whose smooth defensive walls grow straight up from the face of the precipitous rock cliff.

On many occasions, with carefully positioned floodlights directed towards its rugged sides, it resembles, from a distance, a fairy 'Castle in the Air' which could, with some imagination, have stepped out of any Walt Disney fantasy!

Since 1981 the Fireworks Concert has been among the most eagerly awaited events of the Festival, watched by an estimated 250,000 people. At least 100,000 pack Princes Street to see the fireworks launched from the Castle and hear the accompanying music from the orchestra in the gardens below, as cascades of colour light up the night sky.

More than one-and-a-half tonnes of gunpowder go into the display as more than 4,000 rockets, flares, roman candles, mines, shells and other fireworks are used. Each year's show is individually created as bigger and better technology is developed all the time.

The Castle is an excellent backdrop for this event. There are so many different levels and this enhances the show and makes it much more dramatic.

Until 1992 the annual **Hogmanay**[9] (seeing in the New Year) gathering was traditionally held at the Tron Kirk in the High Street. In 1993 however a new venture and venue was established and has become the biggest free

[9]   **Hogmanay** is actually the Scottish name for New Year's Eve. Scots too see out the old year and ring in the new but with different customs. In some areas on Hogmanay many years ago children would dress as they might elsewhere for Hallowe'en and sing carols or dance for favours from their neighbours: 'Rise up good wife and shake your feathers, Do not think that we are beggars, We're just children out to play, Rise up and give us our Hogmanay!' One custom - 'first footin'' - is based upon the belief that the coming year will bring good luck and full larders if a dark-haired person is the first to cross the threshold after the stroke of mid-night carrying a lump of coal or peat and a gift of food to signify plenty, and of course - his

New Year party in the world confirming Edinburgh as the 'World Capital of the New Year'. In that year an estimated 500,000 people squeezed into Princes Street, North Bridge and The Mound to see the Old Year out and the New Year in, in a style which has become one of the Capital's trademarks creating a new Festival along with the long established Summer International Festival. For reasons of safety, however, in subsequent years this number was restricted to about 180,000.

The well-behaved crowds, from many lands, arrive early to take in the vast array of cultural celebrations with shops, restaurants and pubs open, not to mention fairground attractions and atmosphere. Added attractions in recent years have included an open air skating rink set up in East Princes Street Gardens, a huge illuminated Ferris Wheel beside the Scott Monument and festive stalls from Germany at The Mound.

As the bells ring out the dramatic last minutes of the Old Year rhythmic drums along Princes Street give way to a more traditional beat from the pipes and drums and a thundering roar greets the New Year. It soon turns to a chorus of 'oohs and aahs' as a spectacular fireworks display bursts into an orgy of oranges, blues, silvers and golds beamed around the world by the magic of TV and Edinburgh looks its magical best with again the unsurpassed beauty of the Castle – '**Backdrop to Hogmanay**'.

The world famous Edinburgh Military Tattoo, staged annually each August since 1947, is set upon the floodlit natural 'stage' of the Castle's Esplanade. (The word 'Tattoo' apparently comes from the Dutch 'Taptoe', a command given to drummers. Tattoo was also once the bugle signal given to soldiers to order a return to base.) Each year the Tattoo organisers spend £800,000 in erecting temporary seating around the Esplanade for this event. Plans are afoot however for hydraulic seating to be installed turning the event into a state-of-the-art performance arena. The electronic seating would be designed to rise from an underground area at the 'touch of a button'. The cost of the initial construction and installation work would be in the region of £13 million but in time would far outweigh the cost of temporary seating and inconvenience to visitors. However the Tattoo could at some time in the future abandon its traditional site on the Castle Esplanade.

bottle! Where no-one is expected to visit, a dark member of the household might, just before the stroke of midnight, leave the house with a lump of coal and a basket of goodies. At midnight that person would 'first-foot' his own house. Bells ring out throughout the countryside. The Scots Dictionary definition is: 'A New Year's gift; any form of hospitality especially a drink given to a guest to celebrate the New Year or money given to tradesmen and employees on that day e.g. 'Give them their Hogmanay.'

A study of the world-famous event, which attracts more than 200,000 tourists to Scotland, shows proposals to move to a new state-of-the-art arena in Princes St Gardens. More than 1,000 performers take part in the show each night, which has led to fears the castle cannot cope if the programme gets any bigger.

Plans for a purpose-built arena, first discussed in the late 1980s, have been given fresh consideration. The original plans showed how an open-air venue would sit in the shadow of the castle and could be used to host concerts throughout the year. The Tattoo is worth more than £40 million to the Scottish economy.

The highlight of the Tattoo is one which reminds me very closely of a fictitious poem called 'The Last Post', written in 1897 by Dr Ricardo Stephens, about a bugler who died bravely for his country in some foreign campaign but whose ghost returns once a year to the ramparts of the Castle to play his piece. The event at the close of the Tattoo which reminds me of this episode sends a chill down the spines of most spectators who witness it. The lights are dimmed and quickly snuffed out. A solitary piper, high up on the ramparts and lit by a single beam of light, sounds out the sad notes of 'The Last Post' to tell the city below that all is well within the Ancient Fortress. Perhaps he is accompanied by the spectre of a headless drummer who haunts the Castle and was first glimpsed in 1650 by a soldier who heard the slow beat of a drum on the Esplanade! (See page 47)

Let Dr Ricardo Stephens, in his poem from the past, written fifty years before the first Edinburgh Military Tattoo was enacted, paint the vivid picture for us ...

THE LAST POST

(from *Pearson's Magazine* – December 1897).

(Note: Technically there are no buglers in the Highland Regiments, the 'bugle-calls' being sounded by drummers.)

> This is the story, legend, myth,
> Told me in barracks by Drummer Smith,
> Told in Auld Reekie of Bugler Bain[10]
> To the patter and drip of the driven rain,

---

[10] 'Auld Reekie' was the name for Edinburgh's smoky skies in the old days.

While the March wind wailed like a wandering ghost,
And just at the end came the long Last Post.
If you could hear it as told by him,
'twould haunt you 'til death made your eyes grow dim;
And if I could tell it as I was told,
You'd print it on parchment in lettered gold.
The Castle stood grey in the wan moonlight,
Four bugles had rung to the stars 'Goodnight',
They echoed and sang through the old Crown Square,
And whispered away on the ice-cold air.
Then up to the wall went Bugler Bain,
And blew to the East through a port again.
He leant and looked out to the frosty North,
To the hills of Fife and the hidden Forth;
He turned to the East, and he sniffed the sea,
And swore: 'Here's the pick o' the earth to me;
I'd die without winking, if, once a year,
I knew I might play them the Last Post here.'
Or ever the swallows had crossed the sea,
Or the West wind whispered that Spring should be;
An echo of war from the East was sent,
And eastward, far eastward, the bugler went.
He scarce had been tanned by the Eastern sun,
He hardly had seen how a fight was won;
When, straggling a bit on a long hot day,
He came where the enemy's outposts lay;
Who caught him and bound him, and Bugler Bain
Answered the roll-call never again.
They played with their knives 'til his blood ran cold,
They promised him freedom and heaped-up gold,
If, when, to the sound of their hidden tramp
The sleepers awoke in the British camp,
He'd send them confusion and headlong flight,
By sounding 'Retire' through the noisy night.
A shimmer of light as the cold steel stirred,
The bugler was daunted and pledged his word.
That night, for the sentries, the hours went by,
With never a sound but the wolf's weird cry,

Howled down from the hillside, now here, now there,
Now northward, now southward, now everywhere.
Wild faces peered down to the fire-lit plain,
And death-ringed and frowning came Bugler Bain.
Then nearer and nearer the camp they crept,
When up from their clutches the bugler leapt,
White-faced, grim, with a stammered prayer,
He snatched at his bugle and stopped them there;
For out through the silence, sharp and curt,
Rang the rising notes of a shrill 'ALERT'!
Then the bugles sang up, and the rockets rose,
And the whole camp started to greet its foes,
While out from his wounds with a sobbing groan,
Went the Bugler's soul through the night alone.

Four bugles that evening were raised to blare
'Last Post' to the skies from the old Crown Square,
But fifth in the rank ere the call began
Stood the shadowy shape of a dying man.
His cheeks they were white and his lips were grey,
His red-hackled helmet was half away;
His bugle was thrawn, but the notes rang true,
His bugle hand hanging, and half cut through,
His cheek-bone showed bare as he turned his head,
His kharkee coat stained where the blood ran red,
He stood to the left, and he took the word,
And every bugler that bugle heard,
But his stiff, set face, with its staring eyes,
Had the haunting look of a man who dies.
The guard-bugler, stepping toward the wall,
Saw 'That' at his side, but heard no foot fall.
He blew through the port over Castle Hill,
But he felt there was 'That' at his elbow still,
And he heard that for every note he blew,
Instead of one bugle, there sounded Two.
Back to the guard-room four buglers went,
Pale and dry-throated, and ill content;
But Bugler Bain watched the lights o' Leith,

And the Flash-and-Vanish at far Inchkeith,
He went once more all the ramparts round,
While the sentries shivered, and heard no sound.
He harked to the breeze as it whispered by,
From the Pentland Hills came a curlew's cry,
Then he pointed his bugle to Princes Street,
He wailed through the darkness a last Retreat,
And up through the grandeur of Heaven's arch
Went Bugler Bain on his last long march.
All God's winds and the wide world's weather
Met that March night, and fought together;
Blinding snowstorm, sharp sleet, and rain
Beat and battered on Bugler Bain.
Now the mad lightning around him flashed,
Now he stood stunned where the thunder crashed;
A flaring comet went flickering by,
And left him blinded, and choked his cry,
Then up from the earth, came a seething gale,
That caught him, and carried him, breathless, pale,
Where nothing there seemed behind, before,
But blackness and silence for evermore.
He gasped in the stillness, and then he laughed,
True through it all to his well-loved craft;
'Oh! This is the end o' the world,' said he,
'The end o' my bugle, the end o' me;
But, give me a chance, and I'll blow once more
Where never a bugle was blown before.'
He lifted his bugle, he raised his head,
He blew an Assembly 'twould wake the dead.
The darkness was cleft, and the silence rang,
And back with his bugle the Bugler sprang;
For where there was blackness, there came a blaze,
And trumpets sang out from a million ways.
Up through the vastness, pile on pile,
Glittered God's parapets many a mile,
And the rush and the roar of the ranks that rose
Was the sound of the storm where the west wind blows.
Over the ramparts a great voice cried

Strong as the sea in a full spring tide:
'Who is the Bugler who blows so late,
Rousing the Guard at our outer gate?
Who is this braggart who comes so far,
Startling our silence with sounds of war?'
Then point answered and called again,
Shouting in mockery: 'Bugler Bain!'
The wind as it passed him stayed to jeer,
The air grew dark with a nameless fear;
Then all unbidden the swift word sprung
From his trembling lips and his babbling tongue:
'Oh! I was a sinner and lived in sin,
Look to your gates nor let me in.'
There never had risen a word or thought
In the bugler's life, but returned unsought,
And shapes that for years had been underground
Met him and mocked him and hedged him round.
He thought he had shrieked with the damned for aye
Ere ever that laughter had died away.
He bent in the shadow of Hell's own gloom,
And waited in silence to hear his doom.
But while he stood waiting his grim wounds woke
And bled, and the blood as it issued spoke:
'There's many a hundred who scatheless love
To bless the Alarm that he died to give.
These wounds that bear witness, and whence I drip,
Were made ere the bugle had touched his lip,
This bugler tonight had been hale and whole
Had he counted the cost to his perjured soul.'
It ceased, and the thunder rolled out again:
'Ho! Guard of the Drawbridge, pass Bugler Bain!'

So Bugler Bain with his bugle waits
Each night with the guard at the Outer Gates,
'til, up through the darkness, he can hear,
Mounting and murmuring, faint but clear,
From the earthly spot that he loves the most,
The lingering call of the long LAST POST.

Then Bugler Bain blows a swift reply,
And over the City the echoes fly.
But once a year, on a mad March night,
The Bugler returns to his old delight,
For FOUR men come out to the grey Crown square,
To join in the call of the Last Post there;
But FIVE men are seen at the Sergeant's word,
Five bugles that night in the Square are heard,
And two men go up to the outer wall,
Two bugles that night to the eastward call;
But four come again to the 'REVEILLE',
For one, like a shadow, has passed away.

Although the Castle rock is one of the most beautiful, inspiring and historic features of Edinburgh, in the 1960s it was discovered that like most old things it was not as strong as it once was. Time, the elements, traffic, trains, Edinburgh's time-check – the 1 o'clock gun – and even man over the centuries had eroded and weakened it and it began to crumble to the extent of becoming dangerous. Every year three tons of fallen rock were being carried away.

It was a jig-saw puzzle gone wrong; the problem was not how to put it together but how to keep it together. A pot of glue and a few deft brush strokes just didn't add up to enough to keep thousands of tons of rock together but many thousands of pounds were spent in keeping the temperamental rock in its place, considering that it had managed to stand on its own for over 350 million years!

As has been mentioned in an earlier chapter the rock is basalt and a volcanic plug, most of which goes to several miles below the surface, and the surface measures about 10,000 square metres. The basalt has joints or a series of cracks and fissures. If water enters these cracks or joints it may freeze and act as a wedge, causing splintering and breaking-up.

That is what had been happening to the Castle Rock.

To measure movements within the rock delicate seismic devices were set up at various points. About seventy of these 'strain gauges' around the Castle helped to establish where the trouble was likely to occur.

In order to tackle the difficulty the Ministry of Public Building and Works (as it was then) erected a giant spider's web of scaffolding stretching into the sky. Structural engineers and geologists were involved in a study of the rock before work started, special precautions being taken to prevent against rock falls. Everything was worked out in 5 year stages.

The technique used was one successfully used in many countries where city rock structures had needed strengthening e.g. on Sugar Loaf Mountain in Rio de Janeiro.

From the narrow sturdy 'meccano set' scaffolding rust-free bolts were driven 10 ft to 45 ft into the rock to give it something to cling to and ease the strain on the troublesome spots. Resin was inserted into the rock by slight pressure which squelched out, sealing or plugging the fissures. On one occasion they bored 30 ft into the rock and put in 5 tons of cement which the rock absorbed in no time.

The difficulty was obvious. With the rock as a sponge they could not afford to pump too much resin into it. On another occasion, after a 50 ft bore into the rock, water streamed out for 48 hours non-stop. Apparently there are thousands of gallons of water inside the rock.

Because of the Castle's importance as a star tourist attraction the work was carried out in the off-season and scaffolding removed before the tourists arrived. One of the most important aspects of the work was to retain the Rock's ancient appearance, hence the following 'beauty treatment' – before the workmen left the rockface they waterproofed and shaded in the areas on which they had worked leaving cement rock-coloured and rock-shaped and keeping the essential character of the rock. Then, when the tourists arrived they could photograph the rock as it had always been – none the wiser for all the problems it had concealed.

When it was all over Edinburgh Castle was supported by something as solid as a rock!

On reflection perhaps the ghosts of Sir Thomas Randolph, Sir William Douglas, Richard II, the followers of James VI, Oliver Cromwell, the two Argylls and the Jacobite Crusaders must have looked upon such a simple scaffolding with great envy and ponderous thoughts – 'If only we'd a construction like that in our day, how we might have altered the course of history!'

Once a year workers don abseiling gear and hurl themselves over the ramparts to inspect the rocks for problems, ignoring the 250 ft drop below. In the spring of 1997 they identified ledges on the sunny south side where seeds of the rare Scottish plant 'Sticky Catchfly' were planted to take root. This plant was first found in Britain in Holyrood park about three hundred years ago and was becoming extinct until Scottish Natural Heritage successfully reintroduced it.

Series of British Stamps portraying Scottish, English, Irish and Welsh Castles

£1 CARRICKFERGUS CASTLE

£1 CARRICKFERGUS CASTLE

Carrickfergus Castle
Co. Antrim
Northern Ireland
Built between 1180 – 1205
by either John de Courcy
or Hugh de Lacy

£2 EDINBURGH CASTLE

£2 EDINBURGH CASTLE

Edinburgh Castle

£1.50 CAERNARFON CASTLE

£1.50 CAERNARFON CASTLE

Caernarvon Castle
Wales
Built 1283/4 by
Edward I
Completed in present
form 1330

£5 WINDSOR CASTLE

Windsor Castle
Berks
founded by
William the Conqueror
who lived
between 1027 – 1087

Figure 43. 'Photographs' of Edinburgh Castle were sent world-wide

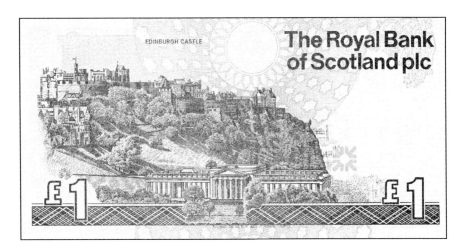

Figure 44. Edinburgh Castle on the reverse of a Royal Bank of Scotland £1 note
(Photograph reproduced by permission of The Royal Bank of Scotland)

To illustrate how popular the Castle was, several years ago a photograph of it was sent world-wide when it appeared on postage stamps valued at £2 each and from 1993 how many people have realised just how much the Castle has been of 'value' since it appeared on the reverse of the Royal Bank of Scotland's £1 notes?

In 1996 on the Bicentenary of Robert Burns the Castle appeared on the reverse of a special Crown piece coin minted for the occasion, and of course for many years confectionery boxes of Edinburgh rock have featured the Castle as their trade mark.

But after centuries of standing firm against marauding invaders, today a silent army marches on the Castle from the main gate unchallenged and armed only with the most recent innovation – a 'CD-Rom' Gallery Guide. This is the state of the art personalised audio system which allows tourists to hook-up and listen-to as they wander through the Castle. For them the *free* electronic guides are an undoubted boon.

Although the Gallery Guide makes use of every sophisticated technology similar to that found in many of today's computers, the visitor end of the system is extremely simple to operate. Throughout the Castle are plaques with a headphone logo and number. By pressing the number on their CD-Rom the visitor can hear information about the part of the Castle they are looking at. The audio tour provides four hours of such information set to one of six languages – English, Spanish, Italian, German, French and Japanese. There are also sound effects and music ranging from traditional Scottish folk song to the Massed Bands of the Military Tattoo.

But with all this progress many people would still wish to talk to a human being, in the shape of a Castle guide, with whom they can have some interaction, and to whom they can direct questions – and of course machines don't crack jokes! During the summer months there are around 200 guided tours a week, stewards leaving with up to fifty people every fifteen minutes.

A security system installed in 1998 caused great difficulties for after-hours tourists in their cars trying to sneak on to the Esplanade to admire views across the Capital. The entrance to the Esplanade is guarded by bollards which sink into the ground for a couple of minutes when legitimate users put in a swipe card to gain access. Tourists trying to dodge in behind a legitimate car which has lowered the bollard have found the bollard popped back up again before they could make it through, damaging the rear of their car.

Until 1998 the Castle just lay empty after the day-time tourists had left, apart from the soldiers garrisoned. Historic Scotland realised there was money to be made from pulling up the Portcullis and inviting people in for some merrymaking. They set up a marketing team to 'sell' the Castle as the perfect place to hold an exclusive dinner dance to celebrate the end of a conference or company success. The price for a big event could be up to £10,000. Most of the larger events are held in the 1000 capacity Jacobite Room – the large modern extension visible from Princes Street. Other smaller rooms like the Gatehouse Suite near the Portcullis can accommodate as few as 15 people for a modest £750.

As part of their night out visitors are given a tour of the Great Hall and shown round the Honours of Scotland Exhibition, featuring the Scottish Crown jewels. Pipers, Highland dancers and even Clan battles can be laid on for the guests.

With its rich and long history and its panoramic views of the city, there can be few more romantic settings for a wedding than the Castle.

But many couples who have wished to wed there have been turned away, either because they don't want to be married by a minister or because their wedding parties have been larger than 40 people.

However in 2004 Historic Scotland launched a huge restoration project to turn a derelict barracks in the Queen Anne building into a wedding venue and applied for a licence to hold civil ceremonies. Besides helping brides to have their dream wedding, this will generate more income. More importantly it will ensure that one of Edinburgh's most important buildings is still a living part of the city.

In recognition of the rate at which the Castle business had grown, however, it was decided in 2000 to move into Executive Management by appointing a 'Castle Commander' in sole charge of co-ordinating all the different uses the Castle is put to – tourism, corporate entertainment, evening functions and so on, and to be more pro-active. This 'Commander' was expected to represent the Castle when dealing with local, national and international organisations and manage day-to-day running as well as looking after Holyrood Park and other city buildings.

Mention was made earlier of the world famous Military Tattoo held on the Esplanade. In March 2000 it went on tour for the first time – thousands of miles away to Wellington, New Zealand! The event formed the centrepiece of the New Zealand Festival 2000 event and featured 280 military musicians from Britain. The mainly Scottish bands 'went down a storm' with all four of their performances being sold out. However they could not try to replicate the Edinburgh Tattoo without having a backdrop of the Castle so they built a replica of it in the stadium in which the Tattoo took place! Invitations have also been received for the Tattoo to be performed in the USA, Canada, South Africa and Australia with the proviso that an exact brick-for-brick replica of the Castle façade be used.

And while on the subject of Tattoos one of the largest to be staged anywhere in the world was held on the Esplanade in July 2000 in celebration of the Queen Mother's 100th birthday. Pipe bands from across the world joined in with up to 600 pipers and drummers taking part.

CHAPTER TWELVE

THE MUSEUMS AND
WAR MEMORIAL

Today the Castle is a respected haven of peace.

The **Scottish Regalia** is the oldest Royal Regalia in Britain comprising jewels of the Crown dated 1540 and Sword of State and Sceptre, made for the Coronations of the Monarchs. It is kept under heavy security in a stone vaulted room, the Crown Room built by James VI in 1617 to house the nation's treasures then in his possession. But those viewing them today perhaps do not realise they had an historic past.

To trace their historic escape and whereabouts we have to look to the north. About one mile north of Inverbervie in Grampian Region lies Old Kinneff Church. This church once concealed the Regalia of Scotland when the minister's wife – Mrs Grainger – courageously smuggled them out of the besieged Dunnottar Castle in 1652 and hid them, from the Cromwellians, below the church floor under the pulpit until the Restoration. A monument there commemorates the action of Mrs Grainger who saved the Honours of Scotland.

An idea prevailed in Scotland that the ancient Regalia had been removed to England, but the novelist Sir Walter Scott obtained permission from the King in London to search for them. Commissioners appointed by the Prince Regent made an examination of the Crown Room at the Castle on 5 February 1818. Nothing was in the room but a large oaken chest. This they directed to be forced open, and it was found to contain the Crown, Sceptre and Sword of State of Scotland in a state of perfect and splendid preservation where they had lain since the Union with England in 1707. The Lord Treasurer's rod of office of silver gilt was there also. As soon as the existence of these precious relics was ascertained the Royal Standard was hoisted and the soldiers cheered, a salute which was heartily echoed from the Castle Hill.

This history of the Scottish Crown Jewels can be discovered in the Honours of the Kingdom Exhibition, which uses colourful tableaux, music and models to tell their story, including how they were buried not once, but twice.

Figures 45 & 46. Scottish National War Memorial

In 1997 the Stone of Destiny took up its place alongside the Scottish Regalia (Chapter 16).

Nearby **The Scottish National War Memorial**, designed by Sir Robert Lorimer and opened on 16 July 1927, consists of a Hall of Honour and a Shrine constructed out of an eighteenth century barracks on the site of the Church of St Mary, once used as an arsenal the exterior of which is severe; the interior is of a rich beauty.

The **Hall of Honour** is lofty with a barrel-vaulted roof supported by octagonal stone columns which form bays, one for each of the twelve Scottish Regiments. Each bay contains a massive volume – the **Roll of Honour** of the relative Regiment. Each day of the year a line of people waits to enter the Shrine and reverently turn the pages of these books. In spite of the constant handling their pages always look pristine, for as soon as a page shows signs of grubbiness or wear it is replaced by a new one, with the names newly written. Indeed, so many come to look and remember, that in this way each book in the Shrine has been renewed every two years since 1927. Like those who shall not grow old in the memories of their loved ones, these pages too will never fade.

It is sad to relate however that during World War One 307 soldiers were executed for desertion or cowardice. Many of them were suffering from shell-shock rather than deliberately seeking to avoid duty. One such case was of a 22 year old Sherwood Forester who was struck down with boils and dysentery and was suffering from shell-shock. When he was ordered 'over the top' to a listening post he refused to go, fearing his constant trembling might give his comrades' position away. His explanation was regarded as insubordination and he was shot dead as a coward by a firing squad in a field in northern France – for a military offence which in civilian life today would seem next to nothing. After many years of campaigning by relatives, however, the names of the 39 Scots soldiers were in 1998 (eighty years after the end of the War) finally recognised and added to the Roll of Honour in the 'Various Corps 1914-1918 Book' to be regarded as war dead, just as certainly as those who had been blown to bits by shells.

Within the Shrine itself the Stone of Remembrance, a solid block of green Italian marble symbolising peace, rests upon an outcrop of the Castle Rock which projects through the floor and bears a steel casket containing the Roll of Honour of the 150,000 Scots who died in the First World War. Over 50,000 of those killed in the Second World

War and later battles have been added to the casket. The following words are carved in stone round the Shrine:

The souls of the Righteous are in the hand of God.
There shall no evil happen to them; they are in peace.

A gigantic oaken figure of St Michael hangs from the roof.

Special mention must be made here of Dr Douglas Strachan, one of the greatest British stained glass artists of modern times, born in Aberdeen in 1875. Among so many of his creations the stained glass windows in the

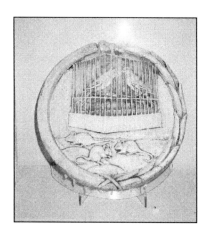

Figure 47. Reproduction cast in the Royal Scottish Museum of the "Tunnellers' Friends" of World War I in the Scottish National War Memorial

Shrine, which are entirely his, might be regarded as his most notable work. They have been praised for their realism and modernity, the absence of conventional symbolism and their factual (often stark) visual records of episodes of the First World War. The studied effect of the transmitted light is something to be experienced and which cannot be conveyed by mere words. It is indeed a fitting contribution to the overall genius of the Shrine's architect, Sir Robert Lorimer. Born in 1864 he grew up eleven miles away from Earlshall at Kellie Castle, the building which inspired his interest in architecture after it was bought by his father. After dropping out of Edinburgh University he studied architecture in London before returning to the City in 1893. Lorimer is often described as Scotland's foremost architect and he was knighted for his work, which includes Dunblane Cathedral and Bunkershill in North Berwick. He also produced several smaller works in Edinburgh ranging from a church in Morningside to suburban villas in St Leonards and Murrayfield and cottages in Colinton. He died in 1929 aged 65.

An interesting feature of the War Memorial relates to a series of circular carvings representing the heads in stone high up in two alcoves as a memorial to many animals which gave their lives and because of their contribution to the various campaigns in the war efforts. These include the heads of a camel, horse, mule, reindeer, dog (with his message tied round his neck), elephant,

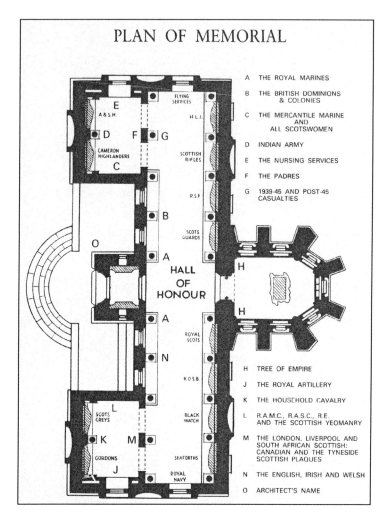

PLAN OF MEMORIAL

A THE ROYAL MARINES

B THE BRITISH DOMINIONS
   & COLONIES

C THE MERCANTILE MARINE
   AND
   ALL SCOTSWOMEN

D INDIAN ARMY

E THE NURSING SERVICES

F THE PADRES

G 1939-45 AND POST-45
   CASUALTIES

H TREE OF EMPIRE

J THE ROYAL ARTILLERY

K THE HOUSEHOLD CAVALRY

L R.A.M.C., R.A.S.C., R.E.
   AND THE SCOTTISH YEOMANRY

M THE LONDON, LIVERPOOL AND
   SOUTH AFRICAN SCOTTISH:
   CANADIAN AND THE TYNESIDE
   SCOTTISH PLAQUES

N THE ENGLISH, IRISH AND WELSH

O ARCHITECT'S NAME

Figure 48. Plan of the Scottish National War Memorial

ram, ox, carrier pigeons and, at a lower level, which interest children, mice and canaries – the 'Tunnellers' Friends' – used for giving warning if the air became unfit to breathe underground; a reproduction cast of this is on display in the Royal Scottish Museum. Carved on the wall is the inscription: 'Remember also the humble beasts that served and died.'

The awe-inspiring beauty of stained glass, wrought steel, sculptured stone and marble of the Memorial as a whole has been described as 'poetry in stone', and is also a fitting memorial to all those historical 'ghosts' back through the mists of time who have been connected with the Castle and its events.

Figure 49. The National War Museum of Scotland

The National War Museum of Scotland. This museum, completely refurbished in 2000, is housed in the former Scottish United Services Museum and adjoining buildings within the Castle walls. Formerly Officers' quarters the original building was erected in 1708 over a vaulted substructure. The museum illustrates a stunning record charting the role of Scotland and the Scots in more than 400 years of warfare from the great historical battles of the seventeenth century to the Falklands War.

More than 2,000 items from the national collection are displayed in six galleries which show the impact of war on the country and its people. Many of the artefacts on show are the touching personal insights of individuals' experience of battle, from family photographs with fatal bullet holes through them to a collection of Victoria Cross medals won for one soldier's bravery.

The museum encompasses the history of all three of the armed services – Army, Royal Navy, Royal Air Force – and civilian reserve forces from the seventeenth century beginnings of professional military service to the present day. It comprises 35,000 distinctive and rare objects, about 2,000 of which are displayed in the six themed galleries explaining military life in war and peace and examines equipment and weapons used and developed by the forces.

One exhibit of interest is a pipe given to a British sergeant by a German soldier during the Christmas truce of the First World War. The pipe – which has a deer's head carved on the bowl and was of the type popular with German hunters – was first presented in a gathering of soldiers from both sides in No Man's Land in December 1914. It was given by a German non-commissioned officer to a sergeant of the 2nd Battalion Scots Guards and later sold to the Regiment's Chaplain, W. H. Abbott, who donated it to the regimental collection after the war. It is one of the very few artefacts to survive from the Christmas Day truce when British and German troops rose from their trenches to play football and sing carols together – only to return to fighting each other hours later!

Another attraction is a £14,000 Grenadier's mitre hat worn by a French soldier on his way to Scotland to join Bonnie Prince Charlie's Jacobite rising.

But an addition of 'more recent' and interesting times is described as follows:

During the living hell of the D-Day Normandy landings of 1944 in World War II a 21 year old piper, Bill Millin, in his kilt and trademark Commando beret, was ordered to play his bagpipes while walking up and down the water's edge, as shells exploded and bullets ricocheted around him, to rouse the spirits of the troops who were coming under heavy fire. While marching ashore he played the tune 'Highland Laddie' followed by 'the Road

Figure 50. Royal Scots Dragoon Guards Museum and Scorpion Tank at the entrance

to the Isles' as men around him perished in the heavy gunfire at Sword Beach. His exploits helped his unit to secure the beach and he continued his piping inland to Pegasus Bridge where paratroopers were awaiting reinforcements. This earned him the title of 'The Mad Piper' – a Scots legend. Bill Millin's heroism was all the more brave as the government of the day had banned pipers from leading regiments into battle because of the terrible number of casualties among pipers during World War I. However the late Lord Lovat, Commander of the famous Commando unit, ignored the rules and ordered Millin to lead the troops ashore.

In 2001 Piper Millin (then 77) donated the historic pipes, kilt, beret and army knife he used that day to the National War Museum. This famous outfit was then to form the centrepiece of a new exhibition on Scotland's links with the Commandos.

On 3 July 1995 Queen Elizabeth opened a new Museum – a proud salute to three historic regiments – commemorating the exploits of the **Royal Scots Dragoon Guards** at the Castle.

A very descriptive article appeared in the July 1995 issue of *Scottish Memories* magazine. With kind permission I quote the following from it:

An Imperial Eagle standard snatched from an elite corps of Napoleon's cavalry by Sergeant Charles Ewart at the Battle of Waterloo takes pride of place in the new Museum.

The Royal Scots Dragoon Guards Regiment was formed in 1971 from the union of two famous regiments, the 3rd Carabiniers and the Royal Scots Greys. The former had themselves been constituted in 1922 from the amalgamation of the old 3rd Dragoon Guards and the Carbiniers (6th Dragoon Guards). The history of the Royal Scots Dragoon Guards is therefore the record of three ancient regiments and, through the Royal Scots Greys, they can claim to be the oldest surviving Cavalry of the Line in the British Army.

The new museum is hard to miss since there is a 6.9 tonne Scorpion Tank parked outside it, indicating the wide range of exhibits celeb-rating the long history of the regiment which dates back to the seventeenth century.

It all began in 1678 when three independent troops of dragoons were raised to quell the Covenanters, that militant body opposed to the enforcement of Episcopacy.

Dragoons of that time were mounted infantrymen armed with

Figures 51 & 52. Royal Scots Greys statue at the edge of Princes Street Gardens

swords and short muskets, the word itself being derived from 'dragon', an old slang term for this particular weapon.

Three years later King Charles II ordered General Thomas Dalyell of The Binns in West Lothian to raise further troops and form them into a regiment to be known as the Royal Regiment of Scots Dragoons, a unit which later was to win world-wide fame as the Royal Scots Greys. At first they were clothed in grey coats and had the grim task of patrolling the fringes of the Highlands. It was not until Marlborough's wars that they finally hit their stride, most notably taking part in a splendid charge at the Battle of Blenheim.[11]

The Jacobite Rebellion of 1715 found them beating the rebels at Sheriffmuir and thrashing Spanish mercenaries at Glenshiel. But it was the Napoleonic Wars that saw their most famous actions.

They fought splendidly with Wellington in Spain. At a critical moment during the battle of Waterloo (1815) the Scots Greys swept on to the massed French forces with the stirring cry of 'Scotland for Ever', the Gordons hanging on to their stirrups. It was at this moment that Sergeant Charles Ewart saw his chance of glory, capturing the Eagle and Standard of the invincible French 45th Regiment after a desperate fight, being later rewarded with a commission from the Prince Regent. In 1936 his old regiment asked permission to have his body exhumed from its Manchester grave and returned to Scotland – Ewart now lies buried on the Esplanade. A memorial stone was erected in his memory in 1938, while the Eagle standard now has pride in a new museum. (The Eagle badge worn by the Royal Scots Greys was derived from this gallant effort.)

[And now a public house in the Lawnmarket – the 'Ensign Ewart' – bears the name of the hero, just a proverbial 'stone's throw' away from his final resting place.]

---

[11] To recognise the valour of the **Royal Scots Greys** an equestrian statue was erected in 1906 where since then it has looked down majestically at the edge of Princes Street Gardens. The statue was modelled on a perfect Army officer - tall, handsome and brave as a lion - Lt Robert Masterton. A fierce patriot, the Edinburgh born soldier had joined the ranks of Scotland's famous cavalry regiment with a powerful sense of duty. He went into the Greys in 1888 aged 20 following in the footsteps of his father and grandfather. It was in South Africa during the Boer War that he had his finest hour. In the battle, the Greys managed to cut off General Cronje's Boer Army at Paardeburg - an honourable victory recorded on the Regiment's Standard. But Masterton never saw the statue - he emigrated to Montreal, Canada before it was erected. He died there in 1961. The statue however has been plagued by bird droppings for many years causing so much damage and corrosion to the bronze surface that in 2000 experts had to give it a coating of special wax to stop future environmental decay.

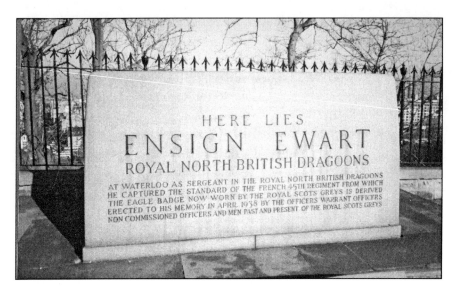

Figure 53. Memorial to Ensign Ewart on the Esplanade

The Scots Greys also took part in the Crimean War although they fortunately missed out on the suicidal Charge of the Light Brigade. However, they did take part in supporting actions including a charge of the Heavy Brigade when two Victoria Crosses were won by Sergeant Major Grieve and Private Ramage.

At the Battle of Balaclava as the famous Thin Red Line of Argylls tried to stave off imminent defeat, the Scots Greys took on a dense mass of Russian cavalry more than 3,000 strong who came galloping over a ridge. The Greys were outnumbered ten to one and charging uphill the ensuing action was one of the most desperate cavalry actions ever seen. Yet the desperate gamble proved successful – the Russians were driven back while the Greys went on to lay siege to Sevastopol.

The First World War found the Regiment covering the British Army's retreat from Mons when they took part in repeated counter-attacks, the last time they were involved in cavalry actions of the old 'charge to the guns' style. Bitter fighting on the Western Front meant they had regiments committed during some of the worst carnage of the war. Their battle honours read like a history of trench warfare – Aisne, Messines, Ypres, Cambrai, Amiens, and the Somme. Casualties were heavy and the 3rd Dragoon Guards had the highest amongst all the British cavalry.

The Second World War saw them fighting in Palestine and Syria and they were involved in the Battle of El Alamein, clearing minefields, forming bridgeheads and taking many prisoners.

The Scots Greys provided the armoured support for the amphibious assault on Salerno on the Italian mainland where fierce fighting continued for ten days almost ending in disaster. If it had not been for the tenacity of the Scots the beach-head might well have been wiped out with horrendous casualties but they survived and fought on, eventually leading a breakout which did not stop until they were walking the streets of Naples.

The Regiment's tanks dipped into the waves that washed the Normandy beaches 24 hours after D-Day and they took part in the bitter fighting at the Falaise Gap which led to a dashing breakout into the French countryside. The Regiment crossed the Rhine on 25 March 1945 and swung north to Bremen which they went on to capture.

In the years since the Second World War the Regiment has served in Cyprus and Northern Ireland. Its most recent active service was in the Gulf War of 1991.

The Regiment now forms part of the Royal Armoured Corps but though horses have been replaced by tanks and armoured cars, it is the cavalry spirit of the past, which provides the inspiration for the future.

In 1995 the Foundation for Sport and the Arts gave the Museum £17,350 for a sculpture of a First World War Dragoon trooper and his horse.

At the opening of the Museum the former Commanding Officer and Colonel of Scotland's only cavalry regiment said, 'We hope our museum will reflect our motto – "Second to None."'

Access to the museum involved negotiating stairs in the Castle, making it difficult for elderly or disabled people. To solve the problem, in 1995 British Telecom gave £17,000 for the installation of a chairlift which runs down the stairs to the entrance.

The Museum co-ordinator said, 'The museum is built on the lower level of the Castle, so the lift is essential for people with disabilities or in wheelchairs. BT's sponsorship means we can offer visitors modern facilities and brings the museum in line with access arrangements for the rest of the Castle.'

Figure 54. Sculpture of a First World War Dragoon
Trooper and his horse within the Royal Scots Dragoon
Guards Museum

Royal Scots Museum. This Regiment (The Royal Regiment) is the oldest in the British Army and as such is the senior Infantry Regiment of the line. It was raised in 1633 when Sir John Hepburn, under Royal Warrant from King Charles I, recruited 1,200 men in Scotland. The first battle honour awarded to the Regiment was Tangier 1680 since when a further 148 have been gained in an history which has involved them in almost every campaign the British Army has fought. The Museum houses paintings, artefacts, silver and medals which tells the regiment's fascinating story from formation to the present day. It is a story which mirrors the fortunes of the country. Whether in Europe, Asia, the Middle East, Africa or the Americas, members of the Regiment have followed the flag in the service of their country.

CHAPTER THIRTEEN

THE JEWEL IN EDINBURGH'S CROWN – A MINI TOUR

To summarise this whole book at this stage let us take a mini-tour of the 'Jewel in Edinburgh's Crown'.

The Castle towers above everything else as Scotland's number one tourist attraction according to the Scottish Tourist Board.

Few visitors leave Edinburgh without having walked up the Royal Mile to the Castle. With over one million visitors each year, more than double the number touring the Queen's home at Buckingham Palace, an independent Consumer research in 1995 praised Scotland's top tourist attraction for offering real value for money at a reasonable price. In 1999 more than 3,500 American tourists voted the Castle as Britain's top attraction in the 1999 Travellers' Choice Award set up by US magazine *British Heritage*.

Every day during the peak of the season thousands of Americans, Japanese and Continentals leave their fleets of air-conditioned coaches and hug their coats or sweaters around them as they step on to the windswept expanse of the Esplanade. There's no place quite like it for the stunning views of the City and the surrounding countryside to be seen from the ramparts, and there's so much to be seen inside.

From many parts of Edinburgh, the Castle always seems to be there, the dominating landmark which has stood for centuries, having been a Royal residence, a centre of administration with a Treasurer's house, Register House and Mint and also an equipment of workshops.

To many visitors the Castle is best known as the home of the annual Military Tattoo, held on its Esplanade during each Edinburgh International Festival.

On entering you cross the drawbridge and pass through the Gatehouse reconstructed in 1888, flanked by statues of Robert the Bruce on the left, who entered the Castle in 1314, and William Wallace, on the right, Scotland's other favourite patriot. The statues were added in 1929. The motto over the Gateway approach reads NEMO ME IMPUNE LACESSIT – 'No one attacks me with impunity'.

The two sixteenth century additions are the Half Moon Battery and the

Figure 55. Gatehouse flanked by statues of Robert the Bruce, on the left, and Sir William Wallace on the right. Over the gateway is the motto 'Nemo Me Impune Lacessit'

Portcullis Gate. The Argyle battery is a good stopping place to look out north over Princes Street, recognised as one of the finest thoroughfares in all Europe, and across the Firth of Forth to Fife.

Nearby is the Mills Mount Battery where each day (except Sunday) the one o'clock gun fires a salute which often takes visitors by surprise but enables locals and tourists alike to check the accuracy of their watches.

In the vault was the fifteenth century siege cannon, Mons Meg, which could fire a cannonball for up to two miles. It is one of the many photogenic gems of the Castle and is now situated near St Margaret's Chapel.

Within the protective walls of Crown Square is the Great Hall, once the seat of the Scottish Parliament, with its intricately carved ceiling and unrivalled collection of armour.

Also in Crown Square is the Scottish National War Memorial, built in 1927 to commemorate the dead of the First World War. There are friezes and a record of the names of 150,000 Scottish soldiers who died in that conflict and in subsequent wars.

Again off Crown Square is the National War Museum of Scotland, an important new military museum, depicting the role of Scottish Regiments in the British Army and graced by weaponry, uniforms and medals. A recent addition, in 1995, is the Royal Scots Dragoon Guards Museum.

Visitors are now admitted to the vaults, where foreign prisoners of war were once held, particularly those captured in the wars with France in the eighteenth/nineteenth centuries. Some of the graffiti scrawled on the walls by the prisoners can still be seen.

In the Crown Room, the highly acclaimed 'Honours of the Kingdom' exhibition features the Scottish Regalia, comprising the Crown Jewels (the crown of Scottish gold, Scottish freshwater pearls, and semi-precious stones from the Scottish mountains, one of the oldest crowns in Europe said to date from Robert I's reign in 1309 but with arches belonging to an even older crown), the Italian Sceptre, donated by Pope Alexander VI to James IV in 1494, and the sword by Pope Julius II to that same king. In 1997 the Stone of Destiny, 'lost' to Scotland for 700 years, took up its place alongside the Scottish Regalia (see Chapter 16).

The oldest building within the Castle precincts is tiny St Margaret's Chapel. Built in the eleventh century it is a popular place for soldiers and their brides in the Edinburgh garrison to be married, and also in which to have their children christened.

There is a restaurant for visitors offering self- and table service, and in 1995, 1997 and 1998 the 'loo' on the Esplanade gained a 'Loo of the Year Award' for being 'Exceptionally well looked after'. At the height of summer, lunchtime means that Castle caterers sell 10,000 packs of sandwiches and 10,000 ice cream cones.

And as an American visitor observed – the Castle was built so very handy to the Railway Station! But what is likely to be of special interest to Scottish people is the fact that for several years past the Castle, like other places of historical interest throughout the country, is open for one weekend FREE of entrance fees!! On one such 'free' weekend in April 1996 more than 18,000 visitors poured through the Castle gates – which is three times the number for a usual paying April weekend.

Since **Sir William Wallace** played such an important part in Scotland's history the visitor will no doubt be interested to learn briefly of the life and epics of the 'Freedom fighter and Hero of a free nation':

William Wallace was born in 1270, the second the three sons of Sir Malcolm Wallace of Elderslie in Renfrewshire. He rose to fame as a guerrilla leader after murdering the Sheriff of Lanark in 1289. His finest hour was the

Battle of Stirling Bridge in 1297 when he joined forces with Sir Andrew de Moray, Lord of Petty in Inverness-shire, to defeat Scotland's governor John de Warenne, the Earl of Surrey and his hated treasurer Hugh Cressingham whose skin was said to have been shared out as a keepsake of the battle.

On 11 October 1297, Wallace wrote to Lübeck and Hamburg in Germany proclaiming Scotland a free nation and was knighted in March 1298 in the name of King of Scots John Balliol.

Wallace was defeated at Falkirk on 11 July 1298, by King Edward I of England, and fled to Europe. He was captured by the English forces in 1305 and executed in London on 23 August that year. His body was divided up and his remains distributed round Scotland towns as a warning to any future rebels.

And we cannot mention Wallace without giving mention to the other Hero:

Robert Bruce – affectionately referred to as Robert 'the' Bruce – (1274-1329) was the grandson of Robert de Bruce (1210-95).

He shared the national rising led by Wallace and soon after the latter's execution in 1305 he rose again against Edward I and was crowned King of Scotland in 1306.

By the Battle of Bannockburn, 24 June 1314, he achieved the independence of Scotland from the English by defeating Edward II and in 1328 the Treaty of Northampton recognised both Scottish independence and Bruce as King. He died of leprosy on 7 June 1329 and was buried in Dunfermline Abbey where his grave is immediately under the pulpit not far from the grave of his Queen Elizabeth and the Shrine of his ancestor, St Margaret. After many centuries his tomb was discovered by chance among the ruins in 1818 and was marked afresh in 1889 by a brass covering. His daughter Marjory married Walter, the High Steward, and from this union came the Royal House of Stewart (or Stuart).

Statues of Wallace and Bruce stand 'on guard' flanking the Gatehouse entrance to the Castle (Figure 55).

CHAPTER FOURTEEN

CASTLE ENTRY FEES –
over the years

After many centuries of English, Scottish and Foreign armies trying to gain 'free' admission to the Castle by means of sieges etc., the authorities which governed the Castle eventually agreed upon a set of charges!

It is interesting to compare the entry fees to the various parts of the Castle and how they have varied over the years of the twentieth century.

The furthest back I can trace is in the *Edinburgh Official Guide of 1929* and quotes the entrance fee to the Castle as 6*d*. (2½p) with Saturdays free. An extra charge of 6*d*. was made for entry to King David's Tower.

No mention was made of entry fees for children at that time.

Moving forward nineteen years to 1948 in the *Edinburgh Castle Official Guide* we find that admission was free to the Castle precincts and the Scottish National War Memorial, but fees for Adults 9*d*. (about 4p) and Children aged 3 to 14 at 3*d*. (about 1p) were made for admission to Historical rooms and the Scottish United Services Museum (now known as the National War Museum of Scotland).

A charge of 6*d*. (2½ p) per person was made for the services of a guide on a conducted tour of the Castle.

In 1960 the same circumstances as above applied but the charges had increased to: Adults 2*s*. (10p) – Children and OAPs 1s. (5p).

In 1996 admission to all parts of the Castle was: Adults £5.50; Concessions £3.50 and Children (5-16) £1.50.

These latter charges of course included the free use of the CD-Rom gallery guide as described in Chapter 11.

Since then charges have increased over the years until in 2004 they are: Adults £9.50, Concessions £7.00 and Children (5-16) £2. No children under 16 will be admitted unless accompanied by an adult.

Nevertheless as has been mentioned in Chapter 13 'an independent Consumer research in 1995 praised Scotland's top tourist attraction for offering real value for money at a reasonable price'.

The **Opening Hours** for Summer are from 1 April 9.30 a.m.-6.00 p.m. with the last ticket being issued at 5.15 p.m. and for Winter from 1 November 9.30 a.m.-5.00 p.m. with the last ticket being issued at 4.15 p.m.

The Castle is closed on Christmas and Boxing Days only.

CHAPTER FIFTEEN

ACCESS FOR THE DISABLED

In their publication *Access Guide for Disabled People* by the Lothian Coalition of Disabled People there is an excellent detailed description for the information of the disabled. I quote from it here since I feel that it is a necessary and most important feature often overlooked in other publications:

PARKING: On the Esplanade except June to September – Parking can be arranged with prior notice for disabled drivers. Telephone 0131 225 9846.

ENTRANCE AND APPROACH: Cobbled uphill driveway from the Esplanade to the interior; long walk.

INTERNAL ACCESS: Disabled people can be transported round the attractions in an adapted chauffeur driven courtesy vehicle which can carry 6 passengers and 2 wheelchairs. Staff assistance available on request throughout Castle complex. Wheelchairs available on loan at various points. Cobbled pathways and roads throughout.

NATIONAL WAR MUSEUM OF SCOTLAND: entrance 3 steps then level on ground floor. Stairlift to first floor. (Alternative ramped access via exit through shop.) Unisex toilet – left/right handrails, 87 cms cubicle door closes with wheelchair inside.

ROYAL SCOTS MUSEUM: One step then level access.

ST MARGARET'S CHAPEL: Viewpoint by the Chapel ramped. Chapel itself up 3 steps, door width 80 cms.

SCOTTISH NATIONAL WAR MEMORIAL: 4 + 3 steps then level. There is a stair-climber for wheelchair access.

GREAT HALL: Ramp available for 4 steps down to Great Hall.

CROWN JEWELS: Access available via ramp to Historic Scotland Offices then lift up to first floor (accompanied by staff only). History in Braille and tactile exhibits.

HISTORIC APARTMENTS: down 3 steps then level access.

TOILETS: Unisex – just inside castle gate, double glass doors. 85 cms cubicle door closes with wheelchair inside, left/right handrails. Kept locked – ask attendant for key. (Toilets also inside café.)

REFRESHMENTS: Café and Restaurant – ground floor, level access, double doors, assistance available. Removable seats at tables. Toilet – café, unisex, level access 90 cms cubicle door closes with wheelchair inside, left/right handrails, alarm cord.

PUBLIC TELEPHONE: In café – level access, coin slot height 121 cms. Two phone boxes near main entrance, not wheelchair accessible.

SHOP: Level access via upper floor entrance (lift to lower floor).

GALLERY GUIDE: (CD-ROM Information System). This system is described in Chapter 11 In addition the audio tour will assist vision – or hearing – impaired visitors. An illuminated screen on the Gallery Guide displays the text of the tour in exactly the same way as the sound recording.

In October 1996 the following letter of appreciation appeared in the local press written by a visitor from Dalmally, Argyll:

> I am a volunteer carer for a severely disabled friend. Last week we realised an ambition of this lady's when we visited Edinburgh Castle. Despite the fact the original architects knew nothing of wheelchairs, every possible effort has been made to be wheelchair friendly. More than that, every member of staff bent over backwards to help us in the most charming and friendly way possible: courtesy car, lifts, ramps, individual attention and a helping push when necessary —all this without any sense of patronage. I would just like to make public our appreciation and thanks to all concerned. LB.

CHAPTER SIXTEEN

THE RETURN OF 'THE STONE OF DESTINY'

On 15 November 1996 an extraordinary journey took place. The historic 'Stone of Destiny' travelled from Westminster Abbey in London where it had remained since Edward I had seized it from the Scots in 1296. It journeyed by Army Land Rover escorted by the Coldstream Guards and crossed the England/Scotland Border to be led by military bands into the small town of Coldstream to a pipe tune composed specially for the occasion and played by Captain Gavin Stoddart (head of Army bagpipe music at the Castle) entitled 'The Return of the Stone'. It was on its way to its new resting place alongside the Honours of Scotland, the Scottish Crown Jewels in the Crown Room of the Castle as being a new appropriate 'tomb' for it. The official Border handover took place on Coldstream Bridge over the River Tweed. On behalf of the Scottish Nation it was accepted by the Scottish Secretary and the Lord Lieutenant of Berwickshire before being carried by two Scottish Regiments – the King's Own Scottish Borderers and the Royal Scots – on the final stage of its journey to Edinburgh.

The Stone then spent a fortnight in the care of Historic Scotland to be spruced up for majestic welcoming celebrations on St Andrew's Day, 30 November 1996. On that day the celebrations were launched by the raising of the Saltire over the Half Moon Battery at the Castle. The Stone was then on view once more. Protected by a Perspex screen it was borne out of the Palace of Holyroodhouse in a specially prepared Land Rover, in ceremonial procession with a mounted escort, along a route lined by thousands of people eager to see history in the making. From Holyroodhouse it was taken first to St Giles' Cathedral for a religious service, where its arrival was inspected by the Duke of York.

Following the service the Stone resumed its journey along the Royal Mile.

On a second leg there was a flypast by four RAF Tornado fighters. Then the formal handover of the Royal Warrant for the safe-keeping of the Stone was made on behalf of the Queen by Prince Andrew, Duke of York and Earl of Inverness, to Scottish Secretary Michael Forsyth and the entrusting of it to the Commissioners of the Regalia.

But what was all this ceremonial about and what was the story behind it?

In the ninth century Kenneth MacAlpin, King of Scots, 'reigned' at Dunstaffnage Castle in Argyll, the original home of the Scottish Kings. He then moved home to Scone (pronounced 'scoon') in Perthshire and with it brought the Coronation Stone or 'Stone of Scone' or 'Stone of Destiny', believed to carry sovereignty, on which all Scottish kings had been crowned.

To trace the history of the stone however we must look back in time to early records which described it as shiny and black covered in writing. It was reputed to be the stone or pillow on which Jacob rested his head while he dreamed his vision of the ladder. In Muirhead's *Scotland* it was 'traditionally identified with Jacob's pillow at Bethel – afterwards the "Lia Fail" or "Stone of Destiny" at Tara in Ireland, or, less improbably, with Columba's pillow on Iona.' In reality it may have been a meteorite, brought to Scotland by migrants heading north from Egypt via Spain and Ireland in ancient times. Drawings show it as having a hollow in which the king could sit while being crowned.

A lecturer in History at Stirling University, Dr Fiona Watson, wrote of it in the *Sunday Post* following the handover ceremony at the Castle:

Whether true or not it is a fact that early Irish Kings were crowned on a stone at Tara. And it is their descendants who are said to be responsible for bringing it to Scotland.

After Roman times the land north of the Tweed was occupied by several peoples – Britons in the south-west, Angles in the south-east, Picts in the north and Scots in the west. The Scots confusingly enough came from Ireland. And it was they who eventually became the dominant people. By the middle of the ninth century they had finally overcome their main rivals the Picts. To emphasise the fact that they now ruled the whole roost they had their man made King on a stone at Scone. Scone had been an important Pictish land so this rammed home the point that the various peoples were now one under the King of Scots. Bringing the ancient stone from Ireland demonstrated the victors' Royal lineage, their right to rule and their connection with an even more distant, not to say holy, past. This was symbolism the peoples of the time would well understand.

Inaugurating a king on a stone was a very old practice in many parts of the ancient world, having associations not just with lineage but with fertility. The Picts themselves would have held similar ceremonies for their own rulers and the significance of the Scots would certainly have hit home.

So the 'Stone of Destiny' was the first unifying symbol of the new Scotland. From then until its theft by Edward I in 1296 it was barely mentioned in any chronicle. It appears on the Seal of Scone Abbey, made in the thirteenth century. But the first literary description of it comes from a Yorkshire chronicler, Walter of Guisborough, after it was stolen. He said it was very large, concave and shaped like a round chair, which doesn't sound like the object that arrived in Edinburgh.

But it doesn't really matter if it is the same stone. It's the symbolism that matters. A thousand years ago it stood for the creation of a new country. After it went to Westminster it became even more powerful standing for a lost nationhood. On its return it served its symbolic purpose yet again. And just as in the ninth century it has been used to try and unite a country – this time Britain. But rather than emphasising the dominance of one people over another the ceremony was designed to show the equality of our relationship with England.

As has already been mentioned Edward I ('Hammer of the Scots') stole the Stone in 1296. He did this in order to demonstrate Scotland's subservience and break Scottish spirit. He carried it off to England, crossing the Border at the town of Coldstream, to remain in Westminster Abbey for the next 700 years. But since everyone knew at the time that Edward I was on his way north to seize the stone would the Scots have sat back and let him steal their most precious possession? The stone he took back to England was a simple square block of sandstone weighing 410 lb which could have been quarried quickly from near Scone. He ordered a Coronation Chair (called St Edward's Chair) to be made of English Oak to hold the stone in Westminster.

Since the reign of Edward II all but two English sovereigns have been crowned on it.

But Edward I was not the only one guilty of having stolen the Stone.

On Christmas Eve 1950 a team of Scottish Nationalists launched a daring raid to recover the Stone from Westminster Abbey. Three young Glasgow students broke in with a jemmy, smashed the front of the Coronation chair and dragged out the historic lump of rock and took it by car to a secret location in Arbroath Abbey. It was eventually returned to London. Since then doubts have been raised that the real stone is hidden safely away somewhere in Scotland and that the version returned was a replica. The leader of the students – Ian Hamilton, now a Scottish QC – stated recently: 'The story went round that we had cheated by returning a fake and hidden the real stone to produce it on some future occasion. The rumour was untrue. We did not play games with the most important single item in the Scottish Regalia.'

But scientific X-ray tests in 1973 showed that metal bolts existed inside the stone. These had been inserted by a Glasgow stonemason after the stone had broken in two when it was removed by the students and before it was returned. The metal rods were taken as proof that the stone was the real thing despite claims it might be a fake. However experts cleaning the historic relic ahead of its delivery to Edinburgh Castle on St Andrew's Day found a tiny hole containing a lead cylinder with a handwritten note inside. It is understood the note, which had at some stage been cut in half, had the letters 'S-C-O' scrawled on it. The message was contained inside the tube thought to have been inserted into the back of the stone by the late Mr Gray, an independent Glasgow Councillor and stonemason.

Mr Gray was believed to have made at least two copies of the Stone, which has thrown doubt over the whereabouts of the genuine article. He was said to have told friends he had placed a secret message inside but never revealed its contents.

A spokesman at the Scottish Office said, 'We can confirm that in the course of conservation work on the Stone a small scrap of paper was found on which a word appeared to be written.' It is believed the Historic Scotland conservationists were unable to decipher any more of the message on the disintegrating paper.

And so the 'Stone of Destiny' which had been 'lost' to the Scottish Nation for seven centuries was lodged securely under the guardianship of Edinburgh Castle side by side with the Honours of Scotland in the Crown Room, available for all to see.

It will however, as occasion presents itself, return to Westminster Abbey at some stage in the future, but only temporarily, for the crowning of Kings or Queens at future Coronations.

EPILOGUE

And so my research is complete.

My 'time machine' has run its course travelling rapidly through many centuries. My knowledge of great events of the past has greatly improved and by putting it all down on paper I hope that it has stirred up an interest in those reading it to visit the scenes for themselves and to let their imaginations wander also.

Over the centuries many writers, known and not so well known, have mentioned the Castle in passing, some in a word to two, others in a few lines.

Here is a selection:

The Castle of Maidens, John of Fordun, 1093

Edinburgh Castle, toune and toure, God grant thou sink for sinne!
And that even for the black dinoir Earl Douglas gat therein.
(Old Ballad on the murder of the young 6th Earl of Douglas at the infamous Black Dinner in the Castle, November 1440, see page 18)

The Castle on a loftie rock is so strongly grounded, bounded, and founded, that by force of man it can never be confounded – John Taylor, 1618

The Castle dominates the town with thunderbolts of war – Arthur Johnston, 1642

Edinburgh Castle, elevated in the air, on an impregnable precipice of rocky earth – Richard Frank, 1658 (My description of 'Edinburgh's Castle in the Air'!)

See yon hoary battlement throned on the rock – James Hogg (the Ettrick Shepherd)

Hark when its sulph'rous vollies fly,
How groans the earth! How roars the sky! – Robert Alves, 1789

Figures 56 & 57. (Above) A view of the Castle from the roof of the Scottish Museum. (Below) An aerial photograph of the setting sun lighting up the Castle and the surrounding landscape – by permission of Alex Hay, Photographer.

My grateful thanks are due to my friend George Weatherstone for his help in scanning all photographs and displaying them in such a professional manner

Such dusky grandeur clothed the height
Where the huge Castle holds its state – Sir Walter Scott

I soon found that the rock contained all manner of strange crypts, crannies and recesses, where owls nested and the weasel brought forth her young – George Borrow (1803-81)

Westward on its sheer blue rock towers up the Castle of Edinburgh – Thomas Carlyle

The Castle has been compared with the Acropolis – Sir John Carr, 1807

The grandeur of Edinburgh depends eminently on the great, unbroken, yet beautifully varied parabolic curve in which it descends from the Round Tower on the Castle Hill to the terminating piece of independent precipice on the north – John Ruskin (1819-1900)

Within the last forty years the Castle Hill was a very narrow ridge. The present Esplanade was not made, there was no enclosure on either side. There was nothing to obstruct the view between the hill and Princes Street. Not a shrub. It was all open – Lord Cockburn 1854

The Castle Rock is, as far as I know, simply the noblest in Scotland conveniently unapproachable by any creatures but sea-gulls or peewits – John Ruskin, 1857

Above all towered the ancient strength of the Castle, battlemented from verge to verge, light as a cloud, insurgent as a wave, massive as its own foundations, etched bold and black against the splendours of the west – S. R. Crockett (1860-1914)

The Castle looked more than ever an hallucination, with the morning sun behind it. Or again it had the appearance of a large canvas scenic device such as surrounds Earls Court – Wilfred Owen

The Castle looms, a fell, a fabulous ferlie, Dragonish, darksome, dourlie grapplan the Rock wi' claws o'stane – Alexander Scott

Aft frae the Fifan coast I've seen Thee tow'ring on thy summit green – Robert Fergusson

The City of romance, Edinburgh. Round its grim rock wars have raged, and alike in its palaces and towers, and under its humblest roofs, poets have dreamed and lovers sung. From its barracks men have marched to make the word Freedom great and holy by the shedding of their blood – Sir Harry Lauder 1927

So long as Edinburgh stands on her hill the Scots will never lack their Jerusalem – John Buchan 1935

The Old Town occupies a sloping ridge or tail of diluvial matter, protected, in some subsidence of the waters, by the Castle cliffs which fortify it to the west, on the one side of it and the other the New Towns of the south and north occupy their lower, broader and more gentle hill-tops. Thus the quarter of the Castle overtops the whole City and keeps an open view to sea and land. It dominates for miles on every side; and people on the decks of ships, or ploughing in quiet country places over in Fife, can see the banner of the Castle battlements, and the smoke of the Old Town blowing abroad over the subjacent country. A City that is set upon a hill – Robert Louis Stevenson (1850-94)

But perhaps we should let that great Scottish Bard, Robert Burns, have the last few words in this selection of quotes. Shortly after he arrived in Edinburgh for the first time in 1786 he penned his 'Address to Edinburgh'. In the three verses I quote he writes warmly of our historic friend.

> There, watching high the least alarms,
> Thy rough, rude fortress gleams afar;
> Like some bold vet'ran, grey in arms,
> And mark'd with many a seamy scar:
> The pond'rous wall and massy bar,
> Grim-rising o'er the rugged rock,
> Have oft withstood assailing war,
> And oft repell'd th' invaders' shock.

With awe-struck thought and pitying tears,
I view that noble stately dome,
Where Scotia's Kings of other years,
Fam'd heroes! had their Royal home:
Alas how chang'd the times to come!
Their Royal name in the dust!
Their hapless race wild-wand'ring roam!
Tho rigid Law cries out, 'Twas just!'

Wild beats my heart to trace your steps
Whose ancestors, in days of yore,
Thro' hostile ranks and ruin'd gaps
Old Scotia's bloody lion bore:
Ev'n I, who sing in rustic lore,
Haply my sires have left their shed,
And fac'd grim Danger's loudest roar,
Bold-following where your fathers led!

And finally let the closing words of the tome *The Story of Edinburgh Castle* echo my own sentiments about *Edinburgh's Castle in the Air*:

Meditating upon the pageant of history which we have endeavoured to recall, the grey towers of the old fortress seem to plead with us to treasure its weather-beaten and war-torn stones as a National monument of the Spirit of Scotland, which would not '**lie at the proud feet of a conqueror**'.

APPENDIX

For those interested in the lineage of the Scottish Monarchs I list the Descendants from the Unification of Scotland to the Union of the Crowns of Scotland and England.

SOVEREIGNS OF SCOTLAND
Celtic Kings

Malcolm II	1005	Edgar	1097
Duncan I	1034	Alexander I	1107
Macbeth	1040	David I	1124
Malcolm III		Malcolm IV	1153
Canmore	1057	William the	
Donald Bane	1093	Lion	1165
Duncan II	1094	Alexander II	1214
Donald Bane		Alexander III	1249
(restored)	1095		

Margaret of Norway 1286-90

English Domination

John Balliol	1292–6	Annexed	1296-
		to England	1306

House of Bruce

Robert I		David II	1329
Bruce	1306		

House of Stuart

Robert II	1371	James IV	1488
Robert III	1390	James V	1513
James I	1406	Mary	1542
James II	1437	James VI	1567
James III	1460	Union of	
		Crowns	1603

In addition to those on page 111 the following is a list of the Sovereigns of England mentioned in this book with the dates of their ascent to the throne:

West Saxon

Edward the
    Confessor   1042

Norman

William I   1066

House of Plantagenet

Henry II   1154
Henry III   1216
Edward I   1272
Edward II   1307
Edward III   1327
Richard II   1377

House of Lancaster

Henry IV   1399

House of Tudor

Elizabeth I   1588

House of Stuart

James I   1603
Charles I   1625
Charles II   1660
James II   1685
Queen Anne   1702

House of Hanover

George I   1714
George IV   1820
William IV   1830
Queen
Victoria   1837

BIBLIOGRAPHY

AA Town and City Guides (Edinburgh 1988)

Access Guide for Disabled People (Lothian Coalition of Disabled People, 1995/96)

Book of the Old Edinburgh Club (T. & A. Constable)

Burns, Robert, *The Complete Works of Robert Burns* (Alloway Publishing)

Daiches, David, *Edinburgh* (Hamish Hamilton)

Edinburgh Castle (HMSO)

Edinburgh Castle – Official Guide (HMSO 1948)

Edinburgh's Official Guide (Edinburgh Corporation 1929)

Evening News, Edinburgh, and Supplements (Scotsman Publications Ltd)

Fairley, A., *The Queensferry Companion* (Albyn Press, 1981)

Gilbert, William, *Edinburgh Life in the 19th Century* (1901)

Grant, *Old and New Edinburgh* (Cassell)

Hardie, A.M.R.,*Close Encounters in the Royal Mile* (John Donald Publishers 1995)

Harper's Handbook to Edinburgh (Noel Collins, 1981)

Hutchinson's Twentieth Century Encyclopaedia (Hutchinson, 1956)

Jarvie, Gordon, *Scottish Castles Activity Book* (HMSO, 1995)

MacGregor, Forbes, *The Story of Greyfriars Bobby* (Ampersand)

Mackenzie, W. Mackay, *The Mediaeval Castle in Scotland* (Methuen 1927)

McLenaghan, *Auld Reekie: A History of Chimney Sweeping* (1987)

Macpherson, A. G., *The Posterity of the Three Brethren* (Clan Macpherson Association – Canada branch)

Muirhead's Scotland (Ernest Benn, 1959)

Pearson's Magazine (1897)

St Margaret Queen of Scotland and her Chapel (St Margaret's Chapel Guild 1957)

Scottish Castles and Fortifications (HMSO)

Scottish Memories Magazine (Lang Syne Publishers)

Slavin, K. & J, *Around Scotland* (Cadogan Books, 1983)

Smith, Charles J, *Historic South Edinburgh* (Vol. 4) (Charles Skilton)

Stevenson, Robert Louis, *Picturesque Old Edinburgh* (Albyn Press)

Story of St Margaret (Historic Scotland pamphlet, 1993)

Sunday Post (D. C. Thomson & Co.)

Turnbull, Michael T. R. B., *Edinburgh Book of Quotations* (1991)

Weirter, Louis, *The Story of Edinburgh Castle* (Harrop, 1913)

INDEX

ABOUT THE AUTHOR

Alastair M. R. Hardie is a retired Welfare Officer of British Telecom who has always had an overall interest in the history of his native City of Edinburgh. This, he says, is probably inherited from his late grandfather, Andrew Gibson Macpherson, who was born in Chessel's Court off the Royal Mile and who took a special interest in the surrounding area leading up to the Castle.

For over forty years, however, Alastair has had an insatiable curiosity into the history of Edinburgh Castle – how old it was; who lived in it; did Royalty play a part in it?; were any battles fought in close proximity to it? And so on. At intervals over the years he has researched it thoroughly and has continued to add to his findings as new items of reference emerged from time to time, and this is the result.

Author of *Close Encounters in the Royal Mile* (1995) – a walking guide to the famous Mile with an historical background to all the closes, wynds, pends and lands including an history of the Nor' Loch – he also, along with his late wife Helen, had another book published in 1991 entitled *Why Me?* being the life story of their daughter Sheenagh, born in 1961 with Down's Syndrome.

His son and daughter-in-law with their three children live in East Kilbride, near Glasgow.